3단어 3문장 3분 영어
A Quartet of Threes

3단어 3문장 3분 영어 A Quartet of Threes

발행일	2025년 12월 5일
지은이	KEETS(키츠) 영어
펴낸이	손형국
펴낸곳	(주)북랩
출판등록	2004. 12. 1(제2012-000051호)
주소	서울특별시 금천구 가산디지털 1로 168, 우림라이온스밸리 B동 B111호, B113~115호
홈페이지	www.book.co.kr
전화번호	(02)2026-5777　　　팩스　(02)3159-9637
ISBN	979-11-7598-012-9 13740 (종이책)　　979-11-7598-013-6 15740 (전자책)

잘못된 책은 구입한 곳에서 교환해드립니다.
이 책은 저작권법에 따라 보호받는 저작물이므로 무단 전재와 복제를 금합니다.
본 도서는 (주)북랩이 보유한 리코 인쇄 장비 등 자체 생산 인프라를 통해 제작되었습니다.

작가 연락처 문의 ▶ ask.book.co.kr
전용 게시판에 문의를 남기시면 저자에게 직접 전달됩니다.

(주)북랩 성공출판의 파트너
북랩 홈페이지와 SNS에서 다양한 출판 솔루션을 만나 보세요!

홈페이지 book.co.kr　•　블로그 blog.naver.com/essaybook　•　출판문의 text@book.co.kr
카톡채널 북랩

영어, 만 3세부터 시작하세요!

3단어 3문장 3분 영어
A Quartet of Threes

KEETS(키츠) 영어 지음

북랩

For my students in KEETS, who are a great joy in my life.

머리말

먼저 이 책이 출간되도록 영어 표현을 감수해 주신 전 서울대 영문과 교수님(Ms. Leah)과 KEETS(키츠)라는 소중한 이름을 지어 주신 30년 경력의 캐나다 방송인(Ms. Adel), 그리고 7Step 특강에 참석해 주신 많은 어머님들께 진심으로 감사를 드립니다.

182권의 영어 동화책에서 활용된 영어 표현들을 모아 이뤄진 이 책이 아이랑 영어로 대화하고 싶은 많은 부모님들에게 도움이 되길 바랍니다.

"영어는 참 어려워요."

"10년 가까이 학교에서 영어를 배웠는데, 나는 왜 영어가 이렇게 어려운가요?"

"미국에 사는 딸(아들)에게 가서 손녀(자)에게 책을 읽어 주고 싶은데, 영어를 못하니 답답해요."

"내 자녀는 나처럼 영어가 불편하지 않았으면 좋겠어요."

"캠프랑 영어 유치원을 알아보다가 비용도 비싸지만 아이에게 좋은 건지 고민하다 왔어요."

"발음도 안 좋고 영어를 아예 기초부터 천천히 배워 보고 싶어서 왔어요."

"해외 주재원으로 가족이 나가는데, 영어를 못하니 남편 없이 현지에서 어떻게 할까 막막해요."

"독서가 부족해서 영어가 더 점프가 안 되는 것 같아요."

"학교에서 영어를 그렇게 했는데, 왜 말 한 마디 못할까요?"

"딸이 직장인이라 손녀(자)를 돌봐야 하는데, 할머니(할아버지)가 영어 교육 시키면 안 될까요?"

"영어 회화 수업은 많이 들었지만, 아이랑 대화하는 표현에는 어떤 말을 해야 할지 모르겠어요."

입시도 끝났고, 번역기가 있고, 좋은 선생님들이 알아서 교육할 거라 생각하니 영어를 공부해야 할 필요성이 없는 시기가 왔습니다. 하지만 일반적으로 30대 부모부터 시작되는 자녀들의 영어 교육 방법에서 수준 차이가 너무 나서 그런지, 요즘은 부모뿐만 아니라 조부모까지 함께 고민하시는 것 같습니다.

유학, 국제학교, 이민, 사립학교, 영어 유치원, 학원, 홈스쿨 등 선택이 너무 다양해지는 시대로 흘러가고 있습니다.

이런 사회에서 "내 아이는?"라고 말하며 걱정하고 조급해 하기보다는 나이에 맞는 양의 언어만 줄 수 있으면 좋겠습니다. 아이들이 공부로 인해 몸이 상하거나 사춘기가 심하게 오지 않았으면 합니다.

'KEETS(키츠)영어'에 오는 학생들이 유난히 선해 보이고, 정성을 쏟는 선생님과 학부모가 일반 학원과 많이 다른 것 같다는 말을 많이 듣습니다.

"선생님! 우리 아이도 책에 실릴 수 있게 작품 만들어 주세요."라는 말씀을 하시며 데려오십니다.

가까이서 지켜본 지인들과 첫 번째 책을 읽고 두 번째 책을 기다린다는 분들의 이야기도 들었습니다. 그래서 그동안 많은 분들이 오셔서 듣고 영어 표현을 질문하셨던 2nd Step 강의 내용을 정리하여 이 책을 출간하게 되었습니다.

세월이 흘러도 다시 보고 싶은 영화를 만들고 싶다던 한 영화감독님의 인터뷰를 보며 '그래 나도 저 마음이었지. 늘 필요한 변하지 않는 영어 표현'을 생각하고 용기를 냈습니다. 이 책을 통해 학원에서 영어 교육이 이루어지기 전에 정서적인 교감이 필요한 '만 3세부터 7세까지 아이들과의 대화를 위한 영어 회화'에 도움이 되길 바랍니다.

2025년 10월 가을에
KEETS(키츠)영어연구소에서

차례

머리말   7

---

1. 책 선정은 신중하게   15
2. Test(나의 영어점수?)   16
3. 유치부 Class   18
4. 나는 특별해요.   21
5. 발음이 걱정이에요   22
6. How to praise(칭찬하기)   23
7. 의성어, 의태어가 너무 궁금해요.   24
8. 동물 이름(아기)   26

A. 아침 준비 끝!   29

1. 눈꺼풀이 부었네   30
2. 물이 미지근해요   32
3. 뒤집어 입었네   36
4. 깨작거리지 마   42
5. 꾸물거리지 마   47
6. 음악하면 너잖아   50
7. 잔소리 좀 그만하세요   53
8. 너 혼난다   60

---

9. 초등부 Class 1   62
10. 초등부 Class 2   65

B. 조잘조잘 방과 후 가족이랑 이야기 나누기   67
  1. 재미없고 지루했어요   68
  2. 팬케이크 먹으렴   72
  3. 공부할 때는 공부하고, 놀 때는 놀자   76
  4. 아빠 단축키 눌러   79
  5. 화가 머리끝까지 났어요   82

C. 심심해요   87
  1. 꼭꼭 숨어라   88
  2. 더 세게 밀어   90
  3. 두껍아 두껍아   92
  4. 동점이야   96
  5. 그림자가 우리를 따라오네   97
  6. 하나 빼기   98
  7. 볼링 하자   99
  8. 슛!   100
  9. 낚았어요!   101
  10. 준비 출발   102

  11. 초등부 Class 3   104
  12. 초등부 Class 4   106

D. 밖에 나가요   109
  1. 올라가는 버튼 눌러   110
  2. 엄살부리지 마!   112
  3. 햄버거 먹으러 가자   121
  4. 배에서 꼬르륵 소리가 나요   123
  5. 피자 먹고 싶은 사람   124
  6. 사진이 흐릿해요   125
  7. 형광펜 사러 가요   127
  8. 난 음치에요   130

9. 가슴이 찡했어요	133
10. 깎아 주세요	136
11. 백억	138
12. 롤러코스터 타러 갈까?	141
13. 주의하세요	144
14. 그 책 빌릴 수 있나요?	146
15. 얼마나 더 가야 되요?	148
16. 보글보글	150

E. 놀아요   161

1. 비눗방울 날려요	162
2. 올림머리 하고 싶어요	163
3. 와르르	165
4. 합체	166
5. 구기지 마	167
6. 물구나무 서	171
7. 막상막하야	177
8. 체인이 빠졌어요	179
9. 꼼짝 마	181
13. 중등부 Class 1	182
14. 중등부 Class 2	184
15. 고등부 Class	186

F. 내일 학교 갈 준비   189

1. 게임 좀 그만해	190
2. 방이 엉망이네	192
3. 식탁에 수저 놓아라	194
4. 정전이에요	195
5. 엄마는 형아 편만 들어요	196
6. 이빨이 흔들려요	201

7. 속으로 읽어   **203**
8. 이 책에 감동 받았어요   **205**
9. 빨래 접자   **207**

G. 사시사철 쓸 수 있는 말   209

1. 안개꽃은 영어로 뭐에요?   210
2. 푹푹 찌네   212
3. 천고마비의 계절   215
4. 진눈깨비가 내렸어요   216
5. 자가용에서   217
6. 지하철에서   218
7. 버스에서   219
8. 기차에서   220
9. 비행기에서   221
10. 애완동물에 대해 이야기할 때   222
11. 스타벅스에서   224

H. 아가에게 영어로 말하고 싶어요   227

I. 뱃속 아가랑 말하고 싶어요   231

16. Daily Children Song   234
17. Korean Children Song   248
18. Answer key   258

에필로그   260

1.
책 선정은 신중하게

자녀가 잘하는 영어 영역을 책으로 더 키워 주세요.

Speaking (말하기)

Writing (글쓰기)

Cracking Problems (문제 풀기)

책 선정은 신중하게

다양한 감성 그림책에서 입시원서 책으로!

순서가 바뀌거나, 건너뛰거나, 잘못 선택하거나, 속도위반은 책 활용의 부작용으로 돌아와요.

이유식을 못한 아이처럼~

2.
Test(나의 영어점수?)

다음 항목의 예시문을 영어로 표현해 보세요. 표현할 수 있는 항목 수에 따라 본인의 영어 실력을 평가해 볼 수 있습니다.

평가 결과는 점수 표를 참고하세요.

01. 코 후비는 아이 / 연필 씹는 아이 / 손가락 빠는 아이
02. 잠꾸러기 / 오줌싸개 / 식사 거르는 아이
03. 눈곱 좀 봐라.
04. 우쭐대지 마.
05. 꾸물거리지 마.
06. 바꿔 신어라.
07. 깨작거리지 마.
08. 성냥 사세요.
09. 고등어, 가자미, 성게, 전복, 낙지, 올챙이
10. 코가 막혔어요.
11. $1 \times 2 = 2$

12. 따뜻하게 입어라.(겨울에 사용)
13. 멜빵, 비니
14. 옹알이하다. / 침 흘리다. / 낙서하다.
15. 살색, 불그스름한, 똥색
16. 그는 코흘리개에요.
17. 미지근한 / 쮸쮸바 / 아이스바 / 고드름
18. 거울아, 거울아. 이 세상에서 누가 제일 예쁘니?
19. 선녀와 나무꾼
20. 보조개 / 주근깨/ 여드름
21. 기차 타라.
22. 서성대지 말고 학교로 똑바로 가.
23. 졸려요
24. 할머니 눈은 왜 그렇게 커요?

표현 항목 수	10개 이하	15개 이하	20개 이하	20개 이상
평가 점수	Fair	Good	Excellent	Perfect

3.
유치부 Class

Every child is a story yet to be told.
모든 아이는 아직 쓰지 않은 이야기다.

* 여섯 살에 만나 책 실컷 보고, 열여섯 살에 외고 영어과 입학.

한 어머님이 KEETS(키츠) 영어 강의를 약 2년 정도 들으시더니, 이렇게 말씀하셨다.

"아이가 생기지 않아 오랜 기도와 기다림 끝에 얻은 소중한 딸입니다. 네 살에 책을 읽어 주니 딸이 저절로 한글 책을 읽어서 영어도 그렇게 하면 안 될까 싶어 왔어요."

그러시고는 여섯 살 따님의 수업을 제안하셨다.

그렇게 여섯 살에 수업으로 만나고 마치기를 열여섯 살.

책을 무척 좋아하며 아이디어가 풍부한 아빠와 단아한 엄마 사이에서 자란 딸은 어떤 모습일까?

아이가 초등 4학년쯤 어느 날, 내게 이런 말을 했다.

"선생님! 다음 출간 책에는 내가 주인공이 되게 해주세요."

그 아이와의 약속을 오늘에야 지키게 되어 기쁘다.

그것도 외고 영어과로 보내게 되어 더 기쁘다.

어릴 때부터 자녀를 예술 쪽으로 키우고 싶다며 전시회를 엄청나게 다니던 모녀.

어려서 공부할 때 집중력이 길지 않을 때쯤 작은 팁을 주니 금방 습관을 바꾸었고, 키즈가 소장하고 있던 거의 모든 책을 읽고 쓰고 맛보고. 한 선배의 Writing을 보여주니 나도 이렇게 쓰고 싶다고 흉내를 내기 시작했다.

또한 스피드가 계속 걸림돌이 될 때쯤 특목고 간 선배 언니가 공부할 때 속도와 집중을 위해 이렇게 했다고 방법을 알려주니 그대로 따라했다. 항상 다음 스텝만 알려 달라고 했던, 자존감이 무척 높던 아이.

어느 날 미술은 내 길이 아닌 것 같다며 내게 말했다.

"모두가 이과를 간다고 나도 꼭 같은 길을 가기보다 내가 잘하는 길을 가면 안 될까요?"

온 가족이 '예술, 문·이과, 국내, 해외, 일반고, 특목고'를 두고 고민하더니, 하나의 길을 선택했다. 이제는 공부의 홀로서기를 하며 집을 떠나 외국어고등학교 기숙사로 갔다. 아마 지금도 열심히 달리고 있을 거다.

책과 학습의 밸런스를 꽤나 맞추며 가끔 공부하기 싫은 날은 둘이서 햇빛놀이, 배드민턴도 하며 참 길게도 함께 달렸다.

주위에서 "어떻게 한 분 선생님께 이렇게 오래 할 수 있느냐?"고 했지만, 외고 길을 선택하고 나니 주위에서 "일찍이 영어과 갈 아이였구나!" 하며 신기하다 했단다.

'책과 입시의 퓨전인 KEETS(키츠)영어' 과정을 다 이루고 보낼 수 있어서 다행이었다. 늘 바쁜 수업으로 지칠 때, 매 학기마다 아이의 영어 100점 소식은 나에게 보람이었다. 이 정도면 고등은 스스로 해도 충분한 아이가 된 듯했다.

그래도 마지막 한 개가 답답하면 고3 끝에 연락하라며 이별했다.

혼자서도 잘 할 거다.

그럴 수 있게 누구보다 열심히 달렸으니까.

4.
나는 특별해요.

언어는 실수하면서 성장합니다.

영어를 가르치기 이전에 이렇게 자신감을 심어 주세요.

I am special

As special as can be

No one in the world is just like me.

나는 특별해요.

세상 누구보다 소중한 존재예요.

이 넓은 세상 그 어디에도 나와 똑같은 사람은 없답니다.

5.
발음이 걱정이에요

이런 문장을 영어로 'Tongue Twister'라고 해요.
한 문장씩 한 주 동안 연습해 보세요.

01. She sells seashells by the seashore.
02. Yellow butter purple jelly red jam black bread
03. Real rock wall real rock wall real rock wall
04. I eat eel while you peel eel.
05. Bitty booty baby bitty booty baby
06. Two tiny tigers take two taxis to town.
07. She said she should sit.
08. Mo mi mo me send me a toe,fe me mo mi get me a mole.
09. I scream ice cream.
10. Eddie edited it.
11. Don't eat with your mouth full.
12. I'll chew and chew until my jaws drop.
13. Spread it thick, say it quick!
14. Sounding by sound is a sound method of sounding sounds
15. Nothing is worth thousands of deaths.
16. Mister kister feet so sweet, Mister kister where will I eat?

6.
How to praise(칭찬하기)

You're a star.	Marvelous!
Super star.	Good job!
Excellent.	Super job!
You're a winner.	Way to go!
Well done.	Cool!
You're the best.	Fantastic!
Good	Incredible!
Perfect.	Wow!
Great	Great work!
Best ever	Looks great!
Bravo!	Much better!
Very well done!	Nice work!
Terrific!	I'm proud of you.
Very good work.	You brighten my day.
Hooray!	You're a joy.
You did it!	You did it!
This is better!	Wonderful!
Awesome	Remarkable!

칭찬해 주서서 감사합니다.

Thank you for your compliment.

7.
의성어, 의태어가 너무 궁금해요.

swish swish	휙휙
woosh woosh	휙, 쌩
rustle rustle	산들산들
tiptoe tiptoe	살금살금
boom boom	쿵쾅쿵쾅
widdle waddle	뒤뚱뒤뚱
gulp gulp	꿀꺽꿀꺽
bang bang	총소리
zzzz	잠자는 소리
ring ring	벨소리
tick-tock tick-tock	시계 소리
twinkle	반짝 반짝
wiggle wiggle	꼼지락 꼼지락
rub-a-dup-dup	둥둥둥(북소리의미)
plippety plop	물방울이 천정에서 또닥또닥 떨어질 때
shoo	(파리에게)저리가
smack	회초리 따위를 휙휙 휘둘러 소리 내다.

screech	박쥐 같은 것이 외마디 소리치다.
buzz	벌 소리
hiss hiss	뱀 움직이는 소리
whoosh	야구공 칠 때
bam	쿵 하는 소리
chu-ga-long-a chu-ga-long-a toot toot	기차 경적 소리
bong	종이 둥 하고 울리다.
pound pound	찰흙이나 밀가루 반죽을 탁탁 치면서
rat-a-tat-tat	둥둥, 꽝꽝 문, 북 따위를 두드리는 연속음
pitter patter	비오는 소리

8.
동물 이름(아기)

동물 이름	아기 동물 or 성별 이름	소리
duck	ducky, duckling	quack quack (squeak)
cow	calf	moo moo
rooster	chick	cock-a-doodle-doo
hen	chick	cluck cluck
dog	puppy	bow wow / arf
dog	puppy	woof / ruff / yip
cat	kitty kitten	meow mew
horse	foal	neigh
pig	piggy piglet	oink oink
goat	kid	baa baa
elephant	elephant calf	stomp (발소리)
wolf	wolf cub	howl
lion/tiger	cub	roar
bear	bear cub	growl
snake	snake	hiss hiss
bird	baby bird	chirp chirp
bird	baby bird	tweet tweet
eagle	eaglet	shriek, cry, screech
goose	gosling	honk honk peep peep

seal	pup	bark
deer	fawn	bell
sheep	lamb	bleet
bat	pup	screech
rabbit/hare/Jackrabbit	bunny	squeak/drum

동물	소리
Ape	gibbber
bat	screech
bear	growl
bee	buzz, hum
bird	chirp, twitter, tweet, sing, whistle
calf	bleat
camel	grunt
cat	mew, purr meow hiss, yowl
cattle	moo, bawl, bellow
chick	cheep

8. 동물 이름(아기)

A.
아침 준비 끝!

1. 눈꺼풀이 부었네

The early bird catches the worm.
일찍 일어나는 새가 벌레를 잡는다.

아침에 아이 깨우느라 힘드시죠?
매일 아침 잠결에 듣는 말이 반복되어
어느 날 아이가 "알았어!"라고 대답할 거예요.

- 아이를 부르는 호칭이 이렇게 많아요.
  Honey, sweetie, sweetheart, pumpkin, buddy, sweet darling
- 일어나 아침이야. / 어서 벌떡 일어나.
  Rise and shine. / Wake up/ The Sun is up.
- 잠꾸러기 / 오줌싸개 / 코흘리개 / 코 후비는 아이
  sleepyhead/bed wetter(betsy wetsy)/snotty nose/nose picker
- 수다쟁이 / 삐짐이 / 멍청이 / 방귀쟁이
  blabbermouth / sulker / butthead / fart monster
- 유치원 갈 시간이야.   **Time for kindergarten.**
- 벌써요?   **Already?**
- 기지개 켜고   **Stretch hard.**
- 눈꺼풀이 부었네.   **Your eyes are puffy.**

- 잠자리 정리해.   Let's make the bed.
- 이불 개라.   Fold your covers(blanket).
- 형아 아직도 자요.   Brother is still sleeping.
- 가서 형아 깨워라.   Go and wake him up.
- 너 아직도 자니?   Are you still sleeping?
- 밤샘 했어요.   I stayed up all night.
- 침 흘렸구나.   You drooled in your sleep.
- 1분만 더 자게 해줘요. 제발.   One more minute mom, please.
- 안 돼, 벌써 늦었어.   No, you're late already.
- 서둘러 안 그러면, 너 늦어.   Hurry up, or you'll be late.
- 금방 나갈게요.   I'll be out in a minute.
- 아침체조하자   Let's do some exercises.
- 이불 덮어   Go under your covers.
- 쌍둥이   twins
  - 일란성 쌍둥이   identical twins
  - 이란성 쌍둥이   fraternal twins
- 그들은 세쌍둥이야.   They are triplets.
- 그는 세쌍둥이 중 한 명이야.   He is a triplet.
- 전업주부   A stay-at-home mom / a full-time home maker

A. 아침 준비 끝!

2. 물이 미지근해요

Turn down the volume. 소리를 낮춰라.
Turn up the volume. 소리를 높여라

먼저 이렇게 짧게 말해 보세요.

· squeeze

· Brush

· up and down, back and forth

· upper teeth, lower teeth

· take a big sip of water.

· Swish, gargle

· spit it

· shiny teeth

- 물 틀어라 / 물 잠가라
  Turn on the water / Turn off the water.
- 세수해라. **Wash your face.**
- 눈곱 좀 봐라. **Look at the sleep in your eye.**
- 얼굴이 부었네. **You have puffy face. Your face is a little puffy.**

- 미끄러워요 It's slippery.
- 뽀드득 손 씻고 Wash your hands squeaky clean.
- 눈에 비누가 들어가서 눈을 뜰 수가 없어요.
  I got some soap in my eyes so I can't open my eyes.
- 말끔히 헹구자. Rinse yourself off.
- 양치질해라. Brush your teeth.
- 화장실 물 내려. Flush the toilet.
- 쉬 할래 / 응가 할래 Do you want to pee or poop?
- 물 내려. Flush the toilet.
- 화장실 네가 들어갈 차례야. It's your turn in the bathroom.
- 칫솔에 물 적셔라. Wet your toothbrush.
- 칫솔에 치약 짜라.
  Squeeze some toothpaste onto your toothbrush.
- 위아래, 앞뒤, 윗니, 아랫니
  Up and down back and forth upper(top) teeth lower(bottom) teeth
- 빛나는 이빨 좀 봐 Look at your shiny teeth.
- 입 헹궈라. 오로록~ Rinse your mouth. Gargle.
- 입안에서 물로 헹궈라. Swish the water around your mouth.
- 뱉어라 Spit it out.
- 칫솔 헹궈라. Rinse your toothbrush.
- 하루 3회 3분 Three times a day for three minutes.
- 입 닦아라. Wipe your mouth.
- 수건 걸어라. Hang it on the towel rack.
- 로션 발라라. Lotion on.

A. 아침 준비 끝!

- 치실을 해요.　　　　　　　I'm flossing.
- 혀 내밀어 / 혀 닦아
  Stick out your tongue./Brush your tongue.
- 입 냄새　　　　　　　　　bad breath
- 발 냄새　　　　　　　　　foot odor
- 물이 미지근해요.　　　　　It's lukewarm.
- 쉬 쌌어요.
  I peed in my pants. (바지에) / I wet the bed. (침대에)
- 휴지로 엉덩이 닦아.　　　Wipe your bum.
- 엄마가 도와줄까?　　　　Shall I help you?
- 엄마가 함께 가줄까?　　　Shall I go with you?
- 소변 보고 싶어?　　　　　Do you want to go pee?
- 눈에 다래끼가 생겼어.　　I have a sty on my eye.

Body part

엄지발가락	big toe	성장통	growing pains
지문	finger print	틀니	false teeth / denture
쌍꺼풀	double eyelid	왼손잡이	left hander / southpaw
겨드랑이	underarm/ armpit		
고양이 같은 수염	whisker		
눈썹	eyebrow	턱수염	beard
속눈썹	eyelashes	콧수염	mustach
종아리	calf	염소 같은 수염	goatee
이마	forehead	다래끼	sty

엉덩이	behind, bottom, seat, butt
얼짱	Good-looking

오후에 아이들이랑 놀 때, 물건 찾기를 해보세요.

"**Where is ~?**"만 해도 아이들이 많은 단어를 재미있게 배울 수 있어요.

Word in the bathroom

비누	soap	칫솔	toothbrush
빗	comb	치약	toothpaste
세면대	basin	손톱깎이	nail clipper
수도꼭지	faucet	면도기	razor
욕조	bathtub	면도날	razor blade
변기	toilet	전기면도기	electric razor
아기 변기	potty	생리대	sanitary pads
거울	mirror	공기 청향제	air freshener
매트	rubber mat	변기 솔	toilet bowl brush
물내리기	flush	전동칫솔	electric toothbrush
배수구	drain	팬	fan
거품	bubble	물티슈	wet tissue
세면대의 물 내리는 손잡이			lever
막힌 것 뚫는 긴 막대 달린 고무			plunger

A. 아침 준비 끝!

3. 뒤집어 입었네

Fine feathers make fine birds.
옷이 날개

- 옷 입어라. / 옷 벗어라. / 갈아입어라.
  Put on your clothes / Take off your clothes / Change your clothes.
- 뭐 입어요?　　　　　　　What should I wear?
- 입을 옷이 하나도 없네.　　Nothing to wear.
- 내 치마 보셨어요?　　　　Have you seen my skirt?
- 이 티셔츠랑 바지 안 어울려.
  This shirt doesn't go well with your pants.
- 더 잘 어울리네.　　　　　It looks better on you.
- 단추 잠가라.　　　　　　Button your shirt/jacket.
- 단추 풀어라.　　　　　　Unbutton your shirt/jacket.
- 단추 잘못 잠갔네.　　　　You buttoned your shirt wrong.
- 앞뒤가 바뀌었네.　　　　 Your shirt is on backwards.
- 뒤집어 입었네.　　　　　Your shirt is on inside out.
- 양말이 짝짝이네.　　　　Your socks don't match.
- 오른발 먼저.　　　　　　Right foot first.

- 다음은 왼발.   Next the left foot.
- 왼발 주세요.   Give me your left foot.
- 소매로 오른팔 그리고 왼팔도 넣어라.
  Put your right arm in the sleeve and your left arm, too.
- 소매 올려 / 내려
  Roll up your sleeves / Roll down your sleeves.
- 일어서서 오른쪽 다리 내밀어 봐.
  Stand up and put out your right leg.
- 들어간다.   In it goes.
- 바지 올려.   Pull up your pants.
- 벨트 고정시켜..   Fasten your belt. / Buckle it.
- 바지 안으로 티셔츠 넣어라.   Tuck your shirt into your pants.
- 지퍼 올려라. / 지퍼 열렸어.   Zip it up. / Your fly is open.
- 등이 보이네.   Your back is showing.
- 속옷이 보이네.   Your underwear is showing.
- 양말 신겨주세요.   Help me put on my socks.
- 신발 신고 끈 매라.
  Put on your shoes and tie your shoelaces.
- 잘못 신었네.   Your shoes are on the wrong feet.
- 바꿔 신어라.   Switch them.
- 주머니에 그것 집어넣어라.   Put it in your pocket.
- 따뜻하게 입어라.(겨울에 사용)   Bundle up.
- 잘 어울리네.   It looks good on you.
- 머리 빗어.   Comb your hair.

A. 아침 준비 끝!

- 나 예뻐 보이지 않아? Don't I look good?
- 가방 들어. Pick up your back pack.
- 내 가방 어디 있어요? Where is my backpack?
- 어제 밤에 여기 뒀는데. I put it over here last night.
- 찾아본 후 엄마를 부르세요.
  Look around first before calling me.
- 구두 정리해. Straighten your shoes.
- 가방 등에 메라. Put your backpack on.
- 버스 놓치겠다, 빨리. You'll miss the bus. Come on.
- 후크 잠궈. Snap it together.
- 셔츠 올려. Pull up your shirt.
- 서두를 필요 없어 There is no big hurry.
- 품위가 있어. You have class.
- 그 옷 입으니까 너무 웃긴다. It makes you look silly.
- 가만있어 봐. Hold still.
- 미니스커트가 유행이야. Miniskirts are in.
- 미니스커트는 한물갔어. Miniskirts are out.
- 유행은 돌고 돌아. Fashion is cyclical.
- 신발이 아직 길지 않았어요.
  My shoes haven't broken in yet.
- 나이에 걸맞게 보인다. You look your age.
- 이 셔츠는 네 흰 피부에 잘 어울려.
  This shirt suits your fair complexion.

- 머리 자르고 싶어요.　　I'd like to get my hair cut.
- 머리 파마 하고 싶어요.　　I'd like to get a perm.
- 드라이로 머리 말려.　　Blow-dry your hair.
- 다리미판　　Ironing board

Types of clothing

한국어	English	한국어	English
멜빵바지	overalls	칠부바지	cropped pants
골반바지	low rise pants	잠옷	pajamas
원피스	dress	반바지	shorts
멜빵	suspenders	팬티스타킹	pantyhose
내복	long underwear, long johns / thermals		
비단 같은	satin, satiny clothes		
실크	silk	속옷	underwear
레이스 양말	Lace stockings	남자 팬티	under pants
트렁크	boxer shorts	프릴 원피스	Frilly dress
목도리	scarf	여자 팬티	panties
겨울 목도리	woolly scarf	조끼	vest
구명조끼	life jacket	비니	stocking cap
체육복	gym uniform	벙어리장갑	mittens
교복	school uniform	정장	business clothes

A. 아침 준비 끝!

Pattern

꽃무늬	floral	체크무늬	checkered
점무늬	polka dot	줄무늬	striped
무늬 없는	plain	단색 빨강 셔츠	solid red shirt
격자무늬	Plaid		

Color

남색	indigo	살색	peach
황토색	tan	하늘색	sky blue
연두색	light green	푸르스름한	bluish
불그스름한	reddish	노르스름한	yellowish

Dialogue

A : How do I look in this dress?
B : It looks good on you. You look younger than your age.
A : I like solid red shirts.

A : 이 드레스 입은 나 어때?
B : 너에게 잘 어울려. 나이보다 어려 보여.
A : 나는 단색 빨간 셔츠를 좋아해.

K : What should I wear, mom?

M : Open the drawers. You can see many clothes.

K : Which pants go better with this shirt, the blue one or the red one?

M : Either will do.

K : Are you sure? In that case, I'll wear this blue one.

M : That's a fine choice.

K : 엄마 뭐 입어요?

M : 장롱 열어 봐. 옷이 많이 있어.

K : 어느 바지가 이 티셔츠에 어울려요, 파랑 혹은 빨강?

M : 둘 중 아무거나.

K : 정말? 그럼 파랑으로 할래요.

M : 잘 선택했어.

4. 깨작거리지 마

A loaf of bread is better than song of many birds.
금강산도 식후경

밥 먹을 때는 어떤 말이 필요할까요?

- 아침 준비 됐어. Breakfast is ready.
- 가요. I'm coming.
- 앉아라. Sit at the table.
- 조심해 뜨거워. Be careful. It's hot.
- 꼭꼭 씹어. Chew it well.
- 천천히 먹어. Take your time eating.
- 깨작거리지 마. Don't be picky.
- 네 몸에 좋은 거야. It's good for you.
- 영양가 있는 거야. It's nutritious.
- 조심해 쏟을라. Watch out you might spill it.
- 먹는 걸로 장난치지 마. Don't play with your food.
- 한 번에 조금씩 먹어. Eat a little bit at a time.
- 엄마 쏟았어요. Mom, I spilt it.

- 제가 닦을게요.   I'll wipe the floor.
- 더 먹을래?   Do you want some more?
- 아뇨 됐어요.   No, thanks.
- 충분하니?   Is that enough?
- 벌써 다 먹었어?   Are you already done?
- 다 먹었어요.   I'm done.
- 나눠 먹자.   Let's share it.
- 의자 집어넣고 물 마셔.
  Push your chair in and drink some water.
- 깨끗이 다 먹어.   Eat everything on your plate.
- 그러고 싶지만 할 수가 없어요.   I'd love to but I can't.
- 많이 먹고 쑥쑥 자라라.   Eat a lot and grow big and strong.
- 아침 준비 됐어. 많이 먹어.   Breakfast is ready. Eat up!
- 골고루 먹어라.   Eat a little bit of everything!
- 한 번에 많이 떠서 먹어 시간 없어.   Eat a lot at one time.
- 골고루 먹어.   Eat a little bit of everything.
- 음식을 태웠어요.   I burned food.

A. 아침 준비 끝!

Caution

아이에게 식사 예절에 대한 말을 영어로 연습해 볼까요?

- 입을 벌린 채 밥을 먹으면 안 돼.
  Don't eat with your mouth open.
- 입에 음식 넣은 채 얘기하지 마세요.
  Don't talk with your mouth full.
- 냅킨을 무릎 위에 두세요.
  Put your napkin on your lap.
- 팔꿈치를 테이블 위에 얹어 놓지 마.
  Don't put your elbows on the table.
- 식사 중에 책 읽지 마.
  Don't read at the table.
- 국물을 후루룩거리면서 마시지 마세요.
  Don't slurp your soup.
- 입에 물고 있지 말고 삼켜.
  Stop holding it in your mouth and swallow.
- 테이블 위에 책을 올려놓지 마. 책에 쏟을 수 있으니까.
  Don't put your book on the table. You might spill something on it.
- 목에 걸리지 않게 조금씩 꼭꼭 씹어.
  Eat a little bit and chew well so you don't choke.
  (your food doesn't get stuck!).
  Bite small pieces and chew, chew, chew!
- 나는 기름기 있는 음식 안 좋아해.
  I don't like greasy food.
- 배가 즙이 많아.   Pears are juicy.
- 군침이 돌아요.   My mouth is watering

Taste

맛있다	yummy	물이 많은	runny
달다	sweet	너무 두꺼운	chunky
쓴	bitter	걸쭉한	mushy
짠	salty	지방 많은	fatty
신	sour	엄청 매운	burning hot
매운	hot	바싹 구운	burned
맵고 짠	spicy	아삭 아삭	crunchy
싱거운	bland	질긴	chewy
기름기 있는	greasy		
맛이 진한	rich		
맛없는	tasteless		
톡 쏘는	tangy		
즙이 많은	juicy		
과일 맛 나는	fruity		
산뜻한	refreshing		
부드러운	soft		
상한	stale, rotten		
딱딱한	solid, not soft		
신선한	fresh		
크림 많은	creamy		
떫은	astringent, tannin		

A. 아침 준비 끝!

flavour

마이구미가 쫀득쫀득(쫄깃쫄깃)	My goomy is chewy.
스프가 걸쭉하거나 묽어요.	Soup is mushy and runny.
치즈케이크가 말랑말랑	Cheese cake is soft.
크래커가 바삭바삭	Crackers are cripsy.
진흙이 찐득찐득	Mud is slimy.
빵이 촉촉	Bread is moist.
젤리가 끈적끈적	Jelly is sticky.
풀이 끈적끈적	Glue is gooey and sticky.
찐득찐득, 끈적끈적	mushy, slimy, sticky
딱딱 / 거친	hard / rough

5. 꾸물거리지 마

Good words cost nothing.
말 한 마디로 천 냥 빚을 갚는다.

외출할 때 꾸물거리는 아이에게 이렇게 해보세요.

- 갈 시간이야.   Time to go. / Let's get going.
- 서둘러 안 그러면 늦어.   Hurry up or you'll be late.
- 차가 기다리잖아.   The bus is waiting for you.
- 준비 다 됐니?   Are you ready?
- 아직 안됐어요.   No, not yet.
- 내 가방 어디 있어요? 여기 놔뒀는데.
  Where is my bag? I put it over here last night.
- 저기 있잖아.   It's over here.
- 비가 올 것 같아.   It looks like it's going to rain.
- 우산 가지고 가.   Take your umbrella.
- 차 조심해.   Watch out for cars.
- 걱정 마세요.   Don't worry.
- 차가 오네.   The bus is coming.

A. 아침 준비 끝!

- 타세요. 내리세요.(버스 / 자동차)
  Get on the bus. Get off the bus. / Get in .Get out
- 먼저 타세요.　　　　　　After you.
- 말썽 부리지 마.　　　　　Be good.
- 운전하시는데 방해 안 되도록 해
  　　　　　　　　　　　Don't distract the driver.
  　　　　　　　　　　　Let's not bother the driver!
- 가방 메고! 출발!　　　　Put on your backpack! Here we go!
- 마치고 집으로 바로 와.　Come straight home after school.
- 재미있게 놀다 와.　　　Have fun.
- 다녀올게요.　　　　　　Bye, mom.
- 꾸물거리지 마.　　　　　Don't procrastinate.
- 놀이방/어린이집/ 유치원/미술수업/야외수업
  Day care center / Nursery school / Kindergarten / Art class / Field trip
- 내 딸(아들) 잘 부탁드려요.
  Take care of my son(daughter),please.
- 몇 반이야?　　　　　　What class are you in?
- 몇 년도에 졸업했어?　　What year did you graduate?
- 몇 학번이야?　　　　　What class are you from?

How to say good bye.

(헤어질 때 하는 말들)

Have a nice day.　　　　Have a great day.

Take care.　　　　　　　See you next time.

See you tomorrow.　　I'm gonna miss you.

See you later.　　　Have a nice trip.

Take it easy.　　　Say hello to your teacher for me.

Dialogue

I'll miss you.　　　　　　　보고 싶을 거예요.

I've grown fond of you.　　정이 들었어요.

I can't quite explain it, but I've grown fond of you.
뭐라고 설명할 수는 없지만, 정이 들었어요.

Words can't express how sad I am.
얼마나 슬픈지 말로 표현할 수가 없어요.

Dialogue

M : Ted, I'll really miss you.

K : Will you really?

M : Yes, I've grown fond of you.

K : What a nice thing to say!

M : 테드, 보고 싶을 거야.

K : 정말요?

M : 네, 정이 들었어요.

K : 고마운 말씀이군요!

A. 아침 준비 끝!

6. 음악하면 너잖아

You're a Jack of all trades!
넌 팔방미인이야.

칭찬은 아이들을 더 잘하게 만들어요.

- 심부름도 잘 하네.　　You're so good at doing errands.
- 너 혼자 다 치웠어?　　Did you clean it up all by yourself?
- 다 컸네.　　You're all grown up.
- 기운 내.　　Cheer up
- 사려 깊기도 하지!　　How considerate!
- 어떻게 그런 생각을 다 할 수가!　How thoughtful of you!
- 믿어지지가 않아.　　Fabulous.(긍정)/ unbelievable.(부정)
- You're a star.　　　　Marvelous!
  Super star.　　　　　Good job!
  Excellent.　　　　　Super job!
  You're a winner.　　Way to go!
  Well done.　　　　　Cool!
  You're the best.　　Fantastic!
  Good　　　　　　　　Incredible!
  Perfect.　　　　　　Wow!

Great	Great work!
Best ever	Looks great!
Bravo!	Much better!
Very well done!	Nice work!
Terrific!	I'm proud of you.
Very good work.	You brighten my day.
Hooray!	You're a joy.
You did it!	You did it!
This is better!	Wonderful!
Awesome	Remarkable!

- 칭찬해 주셔서 감사합니다. Thank you for your compliment.
- 숫자하면 너잖아. You've got a head for figures.
- 음악하면 너잖아. You've got a head for music.
- 그에게 큰 박수 치자. Give him a big hand.
- 손바닥끼리 High five
  바닥으로 탁탁 치기 Low five
  마주보고 정면으로 손 탁 치기 baby five
- 해봐. Go for it.
- 배짱 한 번 좋구나. You've got guts!(긍정) /
  What nerve!(부정)
- 반가운 소식이네. That's good to hear.
- 기회를 잡아. Take a chance.
- 넌 팔방미인이야! You're a Jack of all trades!
- 불가능이란 없다. Anything is possible.
- 비행기 태우지 마세요. Don't put me on.
  Don't flatter me.

- 그는 바이올린에 소질이 있어.
  He has a knack for playing the violin.

- 행운을 빌어　　　　　　　**Break a leg!**

- 내가 얼마나 기쁜지 표현할 수가 없어요.
  I am beyond happy.
  Words can't describe how happy I am.

Dialogue

M : Who is going to accompany your song?

K : Ted's going to play the piano.

M : He has a knack for playing the piano.

K : He really has great chops. He has a natural flair for playing the violin, too.

M : Amazing!

M : 누가 네 노래에 반주할 예정이야?

K : 테드가 할 거예요. 그는 피아노 연주에 소질이 있어요.

M : 그는 재주가 많구나. 그는 바이올린도 아주 잘 켜요.

M : 놀랍구나.

7. 잔소리 좀 그만하세요

What is learned in the cradle is carried to the grave.
세 살 버릇 여든까지 간다.

많은 어머님들이 궁금해 물어보신 잔소리를 모아 보았어요.

- 울음 그쳐.   Stop crying!
- 그만해.   Stop it.
- 진정해.   Calm down.
- 물어뜯지 마.   Don't bite off.
- 밟지 마.   Don't step on it.
- 넘지 마.   Don't step over it.
- 던지지 말고 굴려.   Don't throw, roll it.
- 휘두르지 마.   Don't swing it around.
- 상처내지 마.   Don't get hurt.
- 난폭하게 굴지 마.   Don't be so rough.
- 그것 치지 마.   Don't hit it.
- 입속에 넣지 마.   Don't put it in your mouth.
- 돌아다니지 마.   Don't walk around.

A. 아침 준비 끝!

- 싸우지 마. Don't quarrel with each other.
- 꾸물거리지 마. Don't procrastinate.
- 손대지 마. Hands off!
- 그만 빈둥거려. Stop warming the bench.
- 엄살 부리지 마. Don't be a wimp.
- 비꼬지 마. Don't be sarcastic.
- 잔소리 그만해. Stop nagging.
- 삐쳤니? Are you sulking?
- 맴매한다. I'll spank you.
- 욕심 부리지 마. Don't be greedy.
- 양보해. Give in. / Let him have it. / Let him play with it.
- 말대꾸하지 마. Don't talk back.
- 그만 빈정거려. Don't be sarcastic.
- 범생이 Nerd.
- 생김새 가지고 놀리면 안 돼.
  We shouldn't tease people about how they look.
- 외출 금지 curfew
- 오해하지 마. Don't get me wrong.
- 내려와. Get down.
- 손 떼. Get off me.
- 차 조심해. Watch out for cars.
- 뒤를 잘 봐. Look out behind you.

- 옆을 잘 봐.   Look around you.
- 머리 조심   Watch your head.
- 발밑에 조심해.   Watch your steps.
- 그것 조심해.   Be careful with it.
- 아기 조심해.   Be careful with the baby.
- 상처 나지 않게 조심해.   Be careful not to get hurt.
- 예의를 지켜라.   Mind your manners.
- 조심해서 다뤄라.   Handle it gently.
- 얌전히 있어.   Be gentle.
- 그대로 둬.   Leave it alone.
- 있던 대로 둬.   Leave it as it was.
- 제자리 갖다놔.   Put it back (as it was).
- 그건 못 먹는 거야.   You can't eat that.
- 거기서 내려와.   Get down from there.
- 다섯 셀 동안 그만두는 게 좋을 걸.
  I'm going to count to five, and you'd better stop it.
- 위험하니 버려.   Throw it away, it's dangerous.
- 하나를 보면 나머지는 뻔해.
  You see one, you've seen them all.
- 떨어진다.   You might fall.
- 미끄러진다.   You might slip.
- 머리 부딪칠라.   You might hit your head.
- 손 끼겠다.   You might pinch your hand.

A. 아침 준비 끝!   55

- 데일라.   You might get burned.
- 감기 들겠다.   You might catch a cold.
- 배 아플라.   You might get a stomachache.
- 엎지를라.   You might spill it.
- 젖는다.   You might get wet.
- 더러워진다.   You might get dirty.
- 잃어버리겠다.   You might lose it.
- 앞으로 나와.   Come out to the front.
- 나 좀 빼줘.   Count me out.
- 나 놀리지 마.   Don't pull my leg.
- 비웃지 마.   Don't laugh at me.
- 숙제 미루지 마.   Don't put off your assignment.
- 명심할게요.   I'll keep in mind.
- 핑계 대지 마.   Don't make excuses.
- 징징거리지 마.   Don't whine.
- 엎드려.   Face down.
- 놀리지 마.   No teasing.
- 어렵게 만들지 마.   Don't make it hard.
- 좀 더 큰소리로 말해.   Speak up, please.
- 엉뚱한 말, 쓸데없는 말 하지 마.   Don't talk nonsense.
- 그 말 취소해.   Take it back.
- 우쭐대지 마.   Don't flatter yourself.
- 주절주절 말하지 마(쓸데없이 말이 길어질 때)   Don't ramble.

- 문제를 회피하지 마. 부딪쳐.
  Don't turn a blind eye to the problem. Confront it.
- 주제에서 벗어나지 마. **Don't go off-topic.**
- 요점만 말해. **Stick to the point.**
- 내 말 끝까지 들어. **Hear me out!**
  / Don't speak until I'm finished.
- 집안에서 뛰지 마. **Don't run in the house.**
- 천천히 다녀. **Slow down.**
- 넘어질라. **You might fall down.**
- 서두르지 마라. **Go easy.**
- 알았어요. **Ok, mom.**
- 소파에서 뛰어내리지 마. **Don't jump off the sofa.**
- 다치겠다. **You might get hurt.**
- 그래도 재미있는데. **But it's fun.**
- 그래도 안 돼. **I said no. No menas no!**
- 착한 아이는 그러는 거 아냐. **A good boy does not do that.**
- 여기 할 것과 하지 말아야 할 것 목록이야.
  Here is a list of do's and don'ts.
- 그만해 **Stop it.**
- 기회 한 번만 더 주세요.
  Give me one more chance, please.
- 버릇없이 굴지 마. **Don't be rude!**
- 대꾸하지 마! **Don't talk back!**
- 의자에 엉덩이 붙이고 앉아. **Sit your bottom on the chair.**

A. 아침 준비 끝!

- 분주하게 장난 좀 그만 쳐.   Stop fooling around!
- 거짓말 하지 마, 이야기 꾸미지 마
  　　　　　　　　　　　Don't make a story!
- 그만 뛰어.   Stop jumping!
- 아기처럼 굴지 마.   Don't act a baby!
- 소리 좀 낮춰.   Hold it down!
- 낙서하지 마.   Don't scribble / Don't doodle.
- 하품할 때 입을 가려.   Cover your mouth when you yawn.
- 철 좀 들어라.   Grow up. Time to act your age.
- 시간 낭비 하지 마.   Don't waste time.
- 중얼거리지 마.   Don't mumble.
- 큰 소리로 울지 마.   Don't cry out loud.
- 깜빡거리지 마.   Don't blink.
- 코 골지 마.   Don't snore.
- 우쭐대지 마.   Don't flatter yourself.
- 그 정도는 알았어야지.   You should have known better.
- 예절을 지켜.   Mind your manners.
- 행동 똑바로 해.   Behave yourself.
- 똑바로 앉아.   Sit up.
- 조바심 내지 마.   Hold your horses.
- 숨 좀 돌리자.   Let me catch my breath.
- 내 말 명심해.   Make my words.
- 내 말 듣고 있니?   Do you hear me?

- 두말하면 잔소리죠.   You can say that again.
- 머리 수그려.   Duck your head.
- 변명 하지 마.   Don't make excuses.

8. 너 혼난다

*Train a child in the way he should go,
and when he is old he will not turn from it.*
- *Proverbs* 22:6
마땅히 행할 길을 아이에게 가르치라,
그리하면 늙어도 그것을 떠나지 아니하리라.
- 잠언 22:6

벌을 세울 때 어떻게 말하면 될까요?

• 벽보고 구석에 서 있어.	Stand in the corner.
• 네 방에 들어가.	Go to your room.
• 너 혼난다.	You'll get in trouble.
• 너 벌 받는다.	You'll be punished.
• 머리 위로 손들고 있어.	Hold your hands over your head.
• 됐다 할 때까지 손들고 있어.	Until I tell you put them down.

- 반성했으니까 안아준다.
  Since you're sorry, I'll give you hug.

• 버릇이 없구나.	You're spoiled.
• 보채지 마.	Don't pester.
• 심술 부리지 마.	Don't be so grumpy.
• 징징대며 투정부리지 마.	Don't whine.

- 꼼짝 마.
  Don't go away. / Don't move one inch. / Sit tight. / Stay put.
- 벌 / 칭찬 / 상 / 때리기 / 외출 금지 등의 벌
  punishment / admiration, compliment, reward / spank / grounded
- 너 좀 혼나야겠구나.
  You need to learn a lesson.
- 친구 따돌리는 건 안 좋아.
  It's not good to pick on others.
- 묵비권을 행사하지 마.
  Don't plead the fifth./Don't use your right to remain silent.
- 눈물 거둬.

  Save your tears.
- 너 건성으로 얘기하는구나.

  You are talking half-heartedly.
- 안 된다는 말은 절대 하지 마.

  Never say never.

9.
초등부 Class 1

*Teaching kids to count is fine,
but teaching them what counts is best-Bob Talbert.*
아이들에게 숫자를 세는 법을 가르치는 것도 좋지만,
진짜 중요한 것이 무엇인지 가르치는 것이 더 중요하다.

* 초등 5학년에 만나 책 실컷 읽고, 고1에 영어 1등급, 영어 글쓰기 상, 수학 1등급 받고 연세대(E) 입학.

초등에 공부보다 축구에 빠진 아이.
축구 선수가 되고 싶다며 공만 좋아했던 아이.
그러던 아이가 갑자기 초등 5학년 때, 과학고를 가고 싶다고 한 아이.

엄마가 갑자기 바뀐 아들의 목표에 과학고 견학도 하고, 특목고 설명회도 다니며 길을 찾아다녔지만, 정작 공부가 너무 부족하다 했다. 영유를 다녔지만, 오히려 아들에겐 안 맞았던 것 같다고 했다.

그래서인지 입시 준비를 시키겠다고 조급해 할 초등 고학년이지만, KEETS(키츠)영어를 온전히 믿고 맡겨 주셔서 책을 쌓아 놓고 엄청 읽히고 Writing도 시켰다. 이 아이의 강점은 쓰기보다 말하기를 좋아

했다. 그래서 학교에서 하는 영어연극대회에 참가시키고, 학교 영어 말하기대회에도 참가시키며 흥미를 줄 수 있었다.

친구랑 함께 하는 걸 너무 좋아해서 어려움을 느끼지 않고 도전했다. 덕분에 Speaking 상도 받고, 아이가 마음을 먹으니 금방 속도가 붙었다. 학습 과정에서 문제점이 보일 때마다 아이디어를 제안하면 고집 부리지 않고 망설임 없이 바로 실행했다.

픽쳐, 챕터, 픽션, 논픽션 가리지 않고 읽고, 쓰기를 계속했다.

아이 어머님은, 급하지만 원서와 수능을 같이 시켜 달라고 하셨다. 책과 입시의 퓨전인 KEETS(키츠)영어와 딱 합한 과정이었다.

아이는 그동안 못한 공부를 후회하면서 과학고 목표가 생기자, 수업에서 제시하는 힘든 학습 과정과 숙제를 모두 해냈다. 공부를 하다가 지치고 불안하면 혼자서 동네 운동장에서 축구를 한다고 했다. 게임, 나쁜 친구, 이성을 찾는 그런 아이가 아니라 무척 반듯하고, 시간 숙제 한 번 이탈한 적이 없는 신기한 아이였다.

초등 시기의 넉넉한 시간을 놓쳐서 중학교 3년이 너무 바빴지만, 다행히 고1에 입학 후 2학기 성적표를 보고 담임 선생님이 놀라셨다고 했다.

영어 상장, 국어 글쓰기 상장, 수학 1등급까지 받으며 성장하기 시작했다. 학교 환경에도 영향을 받지 않았고, 학교 점심시간도 아까워 공부에 욕심 있는 한 친구랑 매일 학교 도서관을 다녔다고 했다.

학습 방법을 초등에 많이 익히지 못한 아이라 서툰 학습 때문에 처음에는 많이 힘들었지만, 수업에 와서 선배들 경험을 물어볼 때마다 알려 주자, 스스로 실천해 보며 조금씩 자기만의 방법을 찾아갔다.

과학고는 못 갔지만, 과학고 학생이 꽤 많은 연세대 E과에 합격해 지금 열공 중이다. 대학에서도 전공 강의가 모두 영어로 이뤄지지만 큰 어려움 없다고 한다.

과학고 학생들을 보니 받아들이는 속도가 상당히 빠르지만, 삶에는 수학이 다가 아니니 그들과 서로 융화하며, 똑똑한 친구들 속에서 더 좋은 학습법을 터득해 꼭 성공할 거라 믿는다. 지금까지의 그 노력으로 꼭 기쁜 입사 소식이 들려오길 기대한다.

10.
초등부 Class 2

* 말 없고 조용한 초등 2학년 남자아이. 원서 실컷 읽으며 입시를 준비해 법대에 입학.

초등 2학년인데 아직 영어 단어 읽기가 서툴고, 내성적인 성격이라 집과 밖에서 너무 달라 어렵다며 부탁하셨다. 항상 수업 전에 아이의 성향을 파악하고 마음을 여는 것이 먼저라, 이 아이는 또 어떤 달란트가 있을까 생각했다.

수업 내내 영어 수업인데 농담이나 장난치는 것 없이 질문에만 말을 하고, 책 읽을 때만 목소리를 들을 수 있었다. 그래도 한 번도 KEETS(키츠)영어 가기 싫다는 말도 않고, 아파도 영어 수업은 간다고 하는 것이 신기하다고 아이 어머니가 말씀하셨다.

그러던 어느 날, 아이 어머니가 기쁜 표정으로 얘기하셨다.

"대형 서점을 갔는데, 영어책 코너에서 아이가 이렇게 말했어요!"

"엄마! 나… 이 책들 영어 수업 때 다 읽었어요."

Writing을 처음 시작할 때는 연필을 쥐고 너무 오랫동안 고민을 해서 힘들면 안 해도 된다고 했는데, 드디어 A4 한 장을 채울 만큼 길게 써 내려가는 단계가 되는 걸 보고 나 또한 신기하기도 했다.

그런 그 아이의 한 번 마음먹으면 지독하게 매달리고, 원칙을 지키는 자세를 보며 '법대를 가려나' 했었는데 예상대로 법대 입학 소식을 듣고 깜짝 놀랐다.

'누구나 자기에게 어울리는 곳이 있구나!' 싶었다.

아이들은 각자 잘하는 영역이 있는 것 같다.

Speaking을 좋아하는 E 성향의 아이.

Writing을 좋아하는 I 성향의 아이.

둘 다 중요하지 않고, 100점이 목표인 T 성향의 아이.

모두가 각자 잘하는 요리가 있듯, 영어도 각자 잘하는 영역만 키워주면 되지 않을까 싶다.

B.
조잘조잘 방과 후 가족이랑 이야기 나누기

1. 재미없고 지루했어요

Listen more , Talk less!
적게 말하고 아이 말에 귀 기울여 보서요.

학교 갔다 온 30분! 아이에겐 가장 소중한 시간.
학교에서 있었던 일을 조잘조잘~.
아이의 지친 마음을 읽어 주세요.

- 엄마 저 왔어요. 어디 계세요?
  Mom, I'm home. Where are you?
- 부엌에 있어. / 현관에 있어.
  I'm in the kitche. / I am on the porch.

• 학교 어땠어?	How was school?
• 재미있었어.	Great. / Fun.
• 재미없고 지루했어.	Long and boring.
• 뭐 재미있는 일 없었어?	Anything interesting?
• 특별한 것 없었어요.	Nothing special.
• 그 상처는 뭐야.	What is that scar?
• 누가 너 때렸어?	Did someone hit you?

- 피가 나요.　　　　　　　　　It's bleeding.
- 혹 났네.　　　　　　　　　　You've got a lump.
- 연고 바르자.　　　　　　　　Let's put some ointment on it.
- 떨어졌니? / 박았니? / 베었니?　Did you fall down?
　　　　　　　　　　　　　　／ Did you get hit?
　　　　　　　　　　　　　　／ Did you get cut?
- 살갗이 벗겨졌어요.　　　　　I got a scratch(scratched.)
　　　　　　　　　　　　　　Someone scratched me.
- 시험 어땠어?　　　　　　　　How was your test?
- 쉬웠어요. 한 개 틀렸어요.　　Easy. Only missed one.
- 잘했다.　　　　　　　　　　Good job.
- 망쳤어요.　　　　　　　　　I blew it.
- 수학 낙제 먹었어요.　　　　　I flunked my math.
- 머리 좀 써라.　　　　　　　Shake that brain!
　　　　　　　　　　　　　　／ Use your brain!
- 잘 쳤어요.　　　　　　　　　Perfect.
- 엄마! 날아갈 것 같아.　　　　Mom! I feel like I'm walking on air.
- 이 맛에 엄마가 산다.　　　　It's what I live for.
- 나 녹초가 되었어요.　　　　　I'm worn out.
- 밀린 잠 좀 보충해야겠어요.　I have to catch up on some sleep.
- 수업 빼먹었어요.　　　　　　I missed the class.
- 긴장 풀어.　　　　　　　　　Relax.
- 본론으로 들어가자.　　　　　Don't beat around the bush.
- 무리하지 마.　　　　　　　　Don't overdo it.

B. 조잘조잘 방과 후 가족이랑 이야기 나누기

- 누가 벨을 울려요.   Someone is ringing the bell.
- 내가 나가볼게요.   I'll answer the door.
- 계단을 급히 올라갔더니 숨이 차네.
  I'm out of breath from rushing up the stairs.

Dialogue

Mom : John, How was school?

K : It was a long day. I had an argument with David. What a bummer. I don't understand why he is bad-mouthing me.

M : Really? About what?

K : About my picture. He told me that he said it seemed to be a baby picture. jerk.

Mom : Don't be upset. He's just a big complainer.

Mom : 존, 학교 어땠어?

K : 지루했어요. 게다가 데이빗이랑 싸웠어요. 정말 짜증나요. 난 왜 그가 나를 험담하는지 이해가 안 돼요.

M : 정말? 무엇에 관해?

K : 내 그림요. 애기 그림이라고 나한테 말하잖아요.

Mom : 화내지 마. 그 아이는 그냥 불평이 많은 아이구나 해.

Dialogue

M : What's wrong?

K : I'm out of breath from rushing up the stairs.

M : Why didn't you use the elevator?

K : I was in a hurry and I couldn't wait for it.

M : You shouldn't strain yourself so much.

K : Yeah, I know.

M : 무슨 일이니?

K : 계단을 급히 올라갔더니 숨이 차요.

M : 엘리베이터로 오지 그랬어?

K : 급해서 엘리베이터를 기다릴 수가 없었어요.

M : 너무 무리하지 마.

K : 네, 알겠어요.

2. 팬케이크 먹으렴

The grass is always greener on the other side.
남의 떡이 더 커 보인다.

배고프다는 아이에게 간식을 줄 때, 이런 말을 하면 어떨까요?

- 먼저 손 씻어라.
  First wash your hands.
- 먹을 것 좀 만들어 줄까?
  (Can I) fix you something?
- 주스 좀 마실 수 있어요?
  Can I have some juice?
- 그러고 나서 냉장고 열어 봐.
  And then open the refrigerator.
- 목말라요.
  I'm thirsty.
- 배고파 죽겠어요.
  I'm starving.
- 과자 먹고 싶어요.
  I want to have a snack.
- 과자 대령이오.

Snack is served.

- 너무 많이 먹지 마.
  Don't eat too much.
- 입맛 떨어지니까.
  It'll spoil your appetite.
- 남동생 좀 남겨 줘라.
  Save some for your brother.
- 배고프니? - 조금
  Are you hungry?- kind of.
- 다이어트 중
  I'm on a diet.
- 말하는 건 쉽지.
  Talk is cheap.
- 초콜릿 먹으면 여드름 난다.
  When I eat chocolate ,I break out.
- 낮잠 잘래요.
  I want to take a nap.
- 눈 좀 붙여야겠다.
  I'm going to catch some "z"s.
- 팬케이크에 꿀 발라라
  Put honey on your pancakes.

snack

떡	rice cake	과일 빵	fruit bread
과자	cookies	삶은 달걀	boiled egg
아이스크림 바	popsicle	빵	bread
막대사탕	lollipop	과일	fruit
음료수	beverage, drink	꼬치	skewer
만두	dumpling	과일파이	tart
엿	sticky candy	초콜릿	chocolate bars
고구마	sweet potato	솜사탕	cotton candy
감자	potato	바게트	french bread
시리얼	cereal	죽	porridge

팥빙수	Korean shaved ice dessert topped with sweet red beans
붕어빵	fish-shaped cake with red bean filling
호떡	Korean pancake with sweet filling(Hotteok)
떡볶이	pressed rice cakes and vegetabled in spicy sauce
순대	noodle and vegetable sausage
식혜	Sweet Korean rice punch
삼각 김밥	triangular kim-bab
어묵	Skewered Korean fish cakes in savory broth
찐만두	steamed dumpling

Dialogue

M : What's wrong? You're acting like you're angry.

K : I don't want to talk about it.

M : Something's bothering you. Get it off your chest.

K : Not right now.

M : Ok, but things will be improve if you let it out.

K : Let's have a snack first. Then I'll explain, mom.

M : 무슨 일이야? 뭔가 화가 난 것 같은데.

K : 말하고 싶지 않아요.

M : 뭔가 속상한 게 있구나. 속 시원히 털어놔.

K : 지금은 말구요.

M : 좋아 하지만 말하면 나아질 거야.

K : 먼저 간식 먹어요. 그런 다음 얘기할 게요, 엄마.

속 시원히 말해!

Get it off your chest.(속상한 친구에게)

Open up.(마음 열고 솔직하게)

Speak your mind.(회의에서)

Let it out.(감정이나 생각)

3. 공부할 때는 공부하고, 놀 때는 놀자

If you have problems, open up to me.
무슨 일 있으면 내게 털어놔.

- TV 보기 전에 숙제해.
  Do your homework before you watch TV.
- TV 먼저 보면 안 돼요?
  Can't I watch TV first?
- 내가 좋아하는 드라마가 지금해요.
  My favorite soap opera is on now.
- 안 돼 숙제가 먼저야.
  No, homework comes first.
- 안 된다고 하면 안 되는 거야.
  No means no.
- 엄마 숙제 좀 도와주실래요?
  Can you help me with my homework?
- 물론, 뭐가 필요하니?
  Sure, what do you need?
- 이 문장이 해석이 안 돼요.
  I can't translate this sentence.

- 다했어요.
  I'm finished.
- 그거 암기해.
  Learn it by heart.
- 대충 그 정도~ 끝.
  That's about it. Period.
- 10분만 쉬자.
  Let's take 10 minute break.
- 일할 때는 일하고 놀 때는 놉시다.
  Work when it's time to work, play when it's time to play.
- 보기보다 어려워요.
  It's harder than it looks.
- 선생님이 항상 우리에게 어려운 숙제를 내주서요.
  Our teacher always gives us difficult homework.
- 신경 쓸 게 많아요.
  I have a lot of things on my mind.
- 숙제를 끝내도록 재촉해야겠어.
  I need to push him to get it done.
- 머리를 짜내고 있어요.
  I'm racking my brain.
- 아이가 산만해.
  My child is distracted./My child can't sit still.

Dialogue

M : What's taking you so long?

K : I'm doing my math homework. I have so much homework to do.

M : Is that all?

K : Yes, but it's harder than it looks.

M : What do you mean?

K : It's actually a very difficult assignment. Our teacher always gives us difficult assignments

엄마 : 뭐가 그렇게 오래 걸려?

아이 : 수학 숙제 하고 있어. 나는 할 숙제가 너무 많아.

엄마 : 그게 다야?

아이 : 네, 하지만 보기보다는 어려워.

엄마 : 무슨 얘기야?

아이 : 실제로 매우 어려운 과제거든요. 우리 선생님은 항상 우리에게 어려운 숙제를 내요.

4. 아빠 단축키 눌러

Like father, like son.
부전자전.

- 윤혜랑 통화할 수 있어요? Hello, may I speak to Yoon-hye?
- 전화하신 분은 누구세요? Who's calling, please?
- 끊지 말고 기다리세요. Hold on, please.
- 돌려드릴게요. I'll get her.
- 나갔는데. She's out.
- 언제 돌아올까요? When will she be back?
- 전화 연결이 안 좋아요 We have a bad connection.
- 이제 잘 들려? Can you hear me now?
- 네. Yes, I can hear you.
- 다시 전화할게. I'll call back later.
- 그냥 전화했어요. I just called for no reason.
- 삐 소리가 울리면 메시지를 남겨 주세요.
  After the beep, please leave a message.
- 다른 전화가 왔어요.
  I have another call coming in.

- 통화 중.
  The line is busy.
- 잘 안 들려. 크게 말해 줄 수 있니?
  I can't hear you. Can you speak up?
- 엄마한테 안부 전해줘.
  Say hello to your mom.
  Give my regards to your mom.
- 소리가 멀어지네.
  I'm losing you.
- 연결이 안 좋아.
  We have a bad connection.
- 끊기네.
  Your voice is breaking up.
- 내가 5분 뒤에 다시 걸게.
  I'll call you back in five minutes.
- 시간 있으면 전화해.
  When you have time, give me a call.
- 전화번호가 잘 생각나지 않아.
  I can't remember the phone number.
- 전화가 혼선이야.   The line is crossed.
- 전화 왔어   You've got a call.
                           The phone is ringing.
- 외출 중   She is out.
- 출장 중   She is out of town.
- 잠깐 나갔어요.   She has just stepped out.

- 전화 왔네. 누가 전화 좀 받아줄래?
  The phone is ringing. Would you get it?
- 단축키
  speed dial
- 아빠 오늘은 술 너무 많이 마시지 마세요.
  Daddy, Can you go easy on the drinks tonight?

How to call daddy.

(아빠에게 전화하기)

How about calling daddy?
아빠에게 전화해볼까?

Push the buttons / Dial the number.
버튼 눌러 / 다이얼을 돌려

The line is busy.
통화 중이네.

Let's try again later.
나중에 다시하자.

Say 'hello Daddy, come home early.'
여보세요! 아빠 집에 일찍 오세요.

5. 화가 머리끝까지 났어요

This crisis will pass.
이 어려움은 지나갈 거야.

하루에도 몇 번씩 바뀌는 아이들 기분을 표현해 보세요.

- 기분이 안 좋아 보이네.   You look depressed
  (blue, down, upset)
- 좀 우울해 보이네.   You look kind of blue.
- 짜증 나.   I'm irritated. / I'm annoyed
- 신경이 날카로워졌어.   It got on my nerves.
- 매우 기뻤어.   I was very delighted.
  / I was overjoyed.
- 울고 싶다.   I feel like crying.
- 마음이 아팠어.   I was heartbroken.
- 괴로워.   I was distressed.
- 화났어.   I got mad.
- 기분이 상했어.   I was offended.
- 열 받았어.   It burned me up.
  / It made me mad.

- 기분 나빠. That hurts my feelings.
- 놀라운 surprised

  기쁜 pleased

  헷갈리는 confused

  걱정되는 worried

  겁먹은 scared
- 실망했어. I was disappointed.
- 엄마가 나 실망시켰어. You let me down.
- 시원섭섭해 I was bittersweet.
- 유감이네 It was a pity.
- 창피해 I am embarrassed.
- 당황했어 I was embarrassed.
- 어리둥절하네. I am puzzled.
- 후회된다. I have so many regrets.
- 화가 머리끝까지 났어. I almost hit the ceiling.
- 기가 막혀서 I was stunned. / I was speechless.
- 그 말을 머릿속에서 지울 수가 없어요.
  I can't get it out of my mind.
- 내가 성질부린 거야. I just blew up.
- 내 잘못이야. I was wrong.
- 뻘쭘해. / 어색함을 느꼈어요.
  I feel awkward. / I felt out of place.

B. 조잘조잘 방과 후 가족이랑 이야기 나누기

- 저는 서툴러요. I'm clumsy.
- 모든 것이 잘 될 거야. Everything will be cool.
- 아무 문제없이 지내세요. 걱정 마세요. Stay cool.
- 넌 너무 소심해. You're too timid.
- 가슴이 뭉클했어. I had a lump in my throat.
- 겁내지 마. Don't be a chicken.
- 무슨 말을 해야 할지 몰라 당황. I was at a loss for words.
- 혼자 내버려두세요. Leave me alone.
- 요즘 스트레스를 많이 받아요. I'm stressed out these days.
- 정신 차려. Get real.
- 그냥 화가 나서 엄마에게 화풀이 했거든요.
  I was just angry and I took it out on you.
- 한쪽 귀로 듣고 한쪽 귀로 흘려버려.
  Go in one ear and out the other.
- 기죽지 마세요. Don't be discouraged.
  Don't let it get you down.
  Keep your head up.
  (스포츠나 어려운 상황)
  Don't lose confidence.
  Chin up. (영국식)
- 안절부절 못하겠어요. I'm on pins and needles.
- 정이 들었어요. I've grown fond of you.

Dialogue

M : Why the long face?

K : I failed my finals.

M : Did you study hard?

K : No. As a matter of fact, I hardly studied at all.

M : That's the way it goes. If you don't study hard, you fail.

K : Yes, I'll keep that in mind.

M : 왜 그렇게 시무룩하니?

K : 학기말시험에 낙제했어요.

M : 열심히 공부했어?

K : 아뇨, 사실은 거의 공부를 안했어요.

M: 세상 다 그런 거야. 열심히 안하면 실패하는 거지.

K : 네 명심할게요.

세상 다 그런 거야.

That's the way it goes.

That's life.

That's the way the cookie crumbles.

C.
심심해요

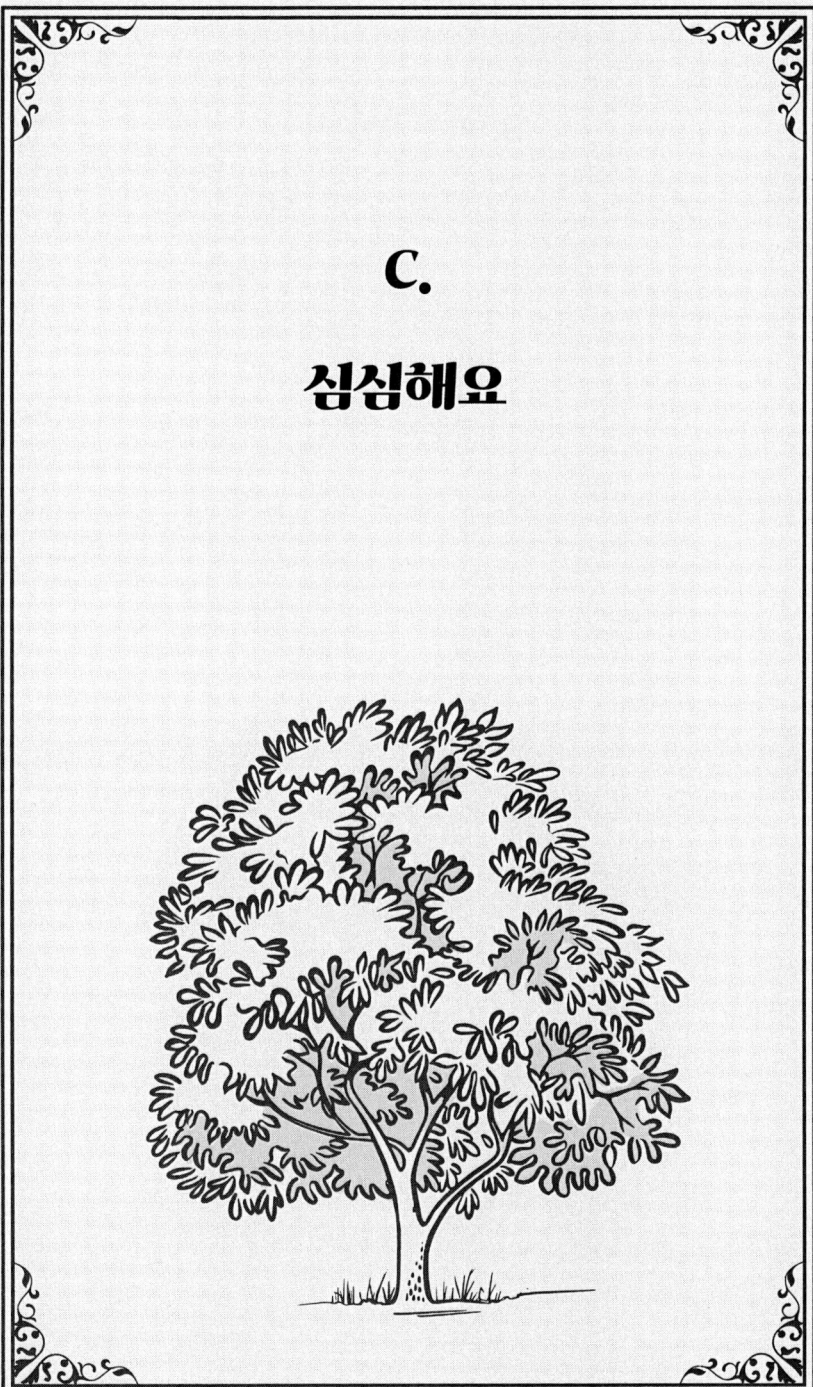

1. 꼭꼭 숨어라

Talent above the talent.
뛰는 놈 위에 나는 놈.

놀이터에서 할 수 있는 말을 살펴볼까요?

- 숨바꼭질하자.
  Let's play hide and seek.
- 재미있겠는데.
  Sounds fun.
- 가위바위보.
  Rock, paper, scissors
- 네가 술래야.
  You're it.
- 10까지 센다.
  I'll count to ten.
- 여기 숨으면 되겠다.
  We can hide in here.
- 꼭꼭 숨어라 머리카락 보일라.
  Come out come out. Wherever you are.
- 준비 됐니, 간다.
  Ready or not here I come.

- 여기 누구 있니?
  Is anybody here?
- 못 찾겠다. 꾀꼬리 마이크를 찾았다.
  Olly Olly Oxen Free! One, two, three, on Mike!
- 포기. 나와라.
  I give up. Come out.
- 내가 이겼다.
  I won.
- 발이 아파 죽겠다.
  My feet are killing me.
- 너무 많이 뛰어서 당연해.
  You ran so much. No wonder!
- 눈 가리고 찾기 놀이 하자.
  Let's play 'Blind man's bluff.'
- 누가 술래 할래?
  Who will be 'it'?

2. 더 세게 밀어

Up you go ; higher and higher.
올라간다. 더 높이.

- 내려와 내가 잡을게.
  Slide down. I'll catch you.
- 무서워요.
  I'm scared.
- 그네에 앉아, 밀어줄게. / 그네에 타(내려).
  Sit on the swing. I'll push you. / Get on(off) the swing
- 더 세게 밀어.
  Push me harder.
- 올라간다. ; 더 높이.
  Up you go ; higher and higher.
- 꼭 잡아, 떨어지지 않게.
  Hold on tight so you don't fall off the swing.
- 그네에서 뛰어내리지 마.
  Don't jump off the swing.
- 친구랑 시소 타라.
  Ride on the see-saw with your friend.
- 올라간다. ; 내려간다.
  Up you go. ; down you go.

- 집에 갈 시간이야.
  Time to go home.
- 친구한테 인사해.
  Say bye to your friend.
- 내일 만나서 또 놀자.
  Let's play together again tomorrow.
- 밖에서 논 다음에는 씻어야지.
  Wash your hands after playing outside.
- 얼굴에 지지가 묻었네.
  You've got some dirt on your face.
- 목덜미도 깨끗이 씻자.
  Let's wash the back of your neck clean.
- 아, 아깝다.
  So close! / What a shame. / That's a shame. / That's unfortunate.
- 아깝다! 이길 뻔했는데
  Oh, so close! You almost won!

  아깝다. 그렇게 열심히 했는데.
  What a shame. You worked so hard.

  아깝다. 단 몇 점 차이였는데.
  What a shame. Just a few points short!

  아깝다. 버스 놓쳤어.
  Too bad! We missed the bus.

  아깝지만 다시 할 수 있어.
  That's unfortunate, but we can try again.

3. 두껍아 두껍아

Don't bury your head.
현실을 도피하지 마.

- 우리 모래놀이할까? Shall we play in the sand?
- 좋은 생각이야. That's a good idea.
- 모래성을 만들자. Let's make a sand castle.
- 삽이 필요해. I need a shovel.
- 여기 있어. Here you are.
- 두껍아 두껍아 헌집 줄게 새집 다오.
  Little toad little toad I'll give you old house. Give me a new one.
- 모래를 손으로 잡으면 다 빠져나가네.
  If I try to hold it in my hands, it all slips out.
- 양동이에 물이랑 모래를 섞자.
  Let's mix some sand and water in this bucket.
- 모래에 모양을 찍자. Let's press this mold in the sand.
- 짜잔. 사과네. Tada! It's an apple.
- 맨발로 걸어 보자. Let's step on the sand with our bare feet.
- 너무 부드러워. It feels so soft.

- 집에 들어오기 전에 발에 묻은 모래 꼭 털어라.
  Shake the sand off your feet before you come in. No sandy feet in the house.
- 그의 얼굴만 알아요.   **I know him by sight.**
- 그의 이름만 알아요.   **I only know his name.**
- 그의 이름은 들어서 알고 있어요.   **I know of him.**
- 그녀 이름을 생각해낼 수가 없어요.
  I can't remember her name.

Dialogue

A : Look at this! I'm making a big sandcastle!

B : Wow! I want to make one too!

A : Okay! Let's make it together.

B : Let's make a big one!

A : Scoop, scoop, scoop the sand! Fill the bucket and flip it over!

B : 1. 2. 3...Tada!

A : Uh-oh! The sand is falling down!

B : It's okay! Let's do it again!

A : If I try to hold it in my hands, it all slips out!

B : The sand is escaping! Haha!

A : Silly sand ! Come back here!

A : 이거 봐! 내가 큰 모래성을 만들고 있어.

B : 와~ 나도 만들고 싶어.

A : 좋아. 같이 만들자.

B : 큰 거 만들자.

A : 모래를 푹푹 푸자. 양동이를 채우고 뒤집자.

B : 하나, 둘, 셋 짜잔!

A : 어머! 모래가 무너지고 있어.

B : 괜찮아! 다시 하자!

A : 손으로 잡으려고 하면 다 빠져나가네.

B : 모래가 빠져나가고 있어! 하하!

A : 장난꾸러기 모래야! 돌아와!

Dialogue

M : Do you know that boy?

K : Yes, he is. That's new student who transferred last week.

M : Oh really?

K : I know him by sight, but his name doesn't ring a bell.

M : 너, 저 아이 아니?

K : 네, 지난주에 새로 전학 온 친구예요.

M : 오, 정말?

K : 나는 그의 얼굴만 알아요. 하지만 그의 이름이 안 떠올라요.

Sports

운동에도 종류가 많죠.

턱걸이	chin-up	준비운동	warm-up
팔굽혀펴기	push-up	기지개	stretch
윗몸일으키기	sit-up	피구	dodge ball
달리기	jog / race	족구	kick ball
줄넘기	skipping rope	잡기 놀이	Playing tag
역기 들기	weightlifting	역기	barbell
레슬링	wrestling	트랙 경기	track and field
3단 경기	triple jump	에어로빅	aerobics
철봉	bar		
테니스	tennis(singles, doubles, mixed doubles)		

야구, 축구, 농구, 배구,
baseball, soccer, basketball, volleyball

정글처럼 생긴 놀이기구
Jungle gym

수영
swimming(freestyle, back stroke, breast stroke, butterfly stroke)

4. 동점이야

The spirit is willing, but the flesh is weak.
마음은 청춘인데, 몸이 안 따라주네

- 동점이야. It's a tie.
- 역전승 Come from behind victory.
- 어느 팀 응원하니? Who are you rooting for?
- 그 게임이 동점으로 끝났어. The game ended in a tie.
- 우리가 7대4로 이겼어. We won 7 to 4.
- 반칙이야. That's a foul.
- 내가 졌어. 오늘은 그만 하자. I lost. Let's stop for today.
- 나 지쳤어. 오늘은 이쯤 하자. I'm exhausted. Let's call it a day.
- 눈 가리고 찾기 놀이 하자. Let's play blind man's bluff.

5. 그림자가 우리를 따라오네

I am the light of my own shadow.
나는 내 그림자의 빛이다.(자신의 내면을 잘 다루어라)

저녁에 작은 불을 켜고 그림자 놀이를 해보세요.

- 벽을 보렴.   Look at the wall.
- 뭔지 맞춰 봐.   Guess what it is.
- 손을 올려 봐.   Raise your hands.
- 손을 내려 봐.   Put them down.
- 새가 되어 보자.   Let's pretend that we are birds.
- 퍼득퍼득   Flap flap
- 팔을 이렇게 뻗어 봐.   Stretch your arms out like this.
- 그림자가 우리를 따라하네. The shadows copy us.

6. 하나 빼기

Sometimes life is just a tie.
가끔 인생은 그냥 무승부다.

- 가위바위보 하나 빼기
  Rock, paper, scissors, take away one.
- 와~ 바위가 가위를 이겼다.
  Wow, my rock wins over your scissors.

7. 볼링 하자

All work and no play makes Jack a dull boy.
일만 하고 놀지 않으면 사람은 지루하고 단조로워진다.

- 볼링 하자.
  Let's do some bowling.

- 저기 핀 10개 보이지?
  You see those 10 pins over there, don't you?

- 공을 굴려서 저것들을 쓰러뜨리는 거야.
  Roll the ball and knock them down.

- 굴려 봐.
  Now roll it.

- 스트라이크. 세 개를 넘어뜨렸어.
  Strike! You knocked them all down.

- 이제 두 개 남았어.
  There are two left.

8. 슛!

Heading for a goal.
목표를 향해 나아가라.

아이랑 가짜 골대를 만들고 놀아 보세요.

- 저게 골대라 하자.
  Let's say that is the goal post.
- 골대를 잘 봐.
  Look at the goal post.
- 그리고 저 사이로 공을 차는 거야.
  And kick the ball between them.
- 슛! 아~ 안 들어갔네.
  Shoot! Ah~ I missed.

9. 낚았어요!

There's always a bigger fish. -Star Wars
항상 더 큰 물고기가 있다 -스타워즈

집에서 아이랑 놀아 보세요.

- 우리는 지금 어부야. Let's pretend we are fishermen.
- 의자에 앉아. Sit on the chair.
- 이 낚싯대를 잡아. Hold the fishing rod.
- 바닥은 강이야. The floor is the river.
- 물에 물고기가 정말 많네. There are lots of fish in the water.
- 한번 낚아 보자. Let's catch them.
- 낚았어요. I caught it.
- 낙지, 문어, 상어, 고래, 가재
  small octopus, octopus, shark, whale, lobster
- 이번에는 낙지를 잡아 봐. Catch the small octopus this time.
- 잘 잡았네. Nice catcher!
- 낚시 정말 잘하네. You are good at fishing.

10. 준비 출발

Keep moving forward. -Walt Disney
계속 앞으로 나아가라. -월트 디즈니

- 우리 자동차 경주 할까?
  Shall we play a car racing game?

- 아빠는 이 자동차로 해야지.
  Dad will use this car.

- 나는 이 소방차로 할래요.
  I'll use this fire engine.

- 이게 출발선이야.
  This is the start line.

- 출발선에 서고 준비 출발!
  On your mark, get set, go!

- 준비됐나요, 선수?
  Are you ready, racer?

- 아빠 차랑 내 차가 부딪쳤어요.
  My dad's car bumped into my car.

- 너무 가까이 오지 마요.
  Don't come too close.

- 이제 간다. 시작이야. 끝장낼게.
  Check check ..Boom!

Dialogue

A : Ladies and gentleman, start your engines! Are you ready, racer?

B : Yes, I'm ready!

A : Okay, here we go! Check check. Boom! Go go go!

B : Vroom! I'm racing! Zoom zoom!

A : 신사숙녀 여러분, 엔진을 켜 주세요! 준비됐나요, 선수?

B : 네 준비됐어요.

A : 좋아요, 이제 시작합니다. 채칵채칵. 펑! 출발!

B : 부릉! 나 달리고 있어요! 슝슝!

11.
초등부 Class 3

* 미술을 좋아하는 초등 3학년. 원서 책과 마음껏 놀고 예고 미술과로 입학.

영유를 졸업하고 사립학교라 영어 수업이 병행되지만 책읽기가 부족하다며 첫째 딸(초등5학년) 수업을 해보시더니, 둘째 딸은 바로 KEETS(키츠) 영어 수업을 시작해 주실수 있겠냐고 하셨다. 큰딸을 보니 Writing이 되려면 책이 꼭 필요한 것 같다며 과감하게 결정을 하셨다. 그러면서 어머니는 이렇게 말씀하셨다.

"둘 다 내 딸이지만, 둘이 성향은 많이 달라요."

수업해 보니 씩씩한 큰딸은 책보다 Speaking이 편했고, 둘째 딸은 책을 엄청 좋아하고 글로 표현하고 그리기를 좋아했다. 선생님이 있든 없든 그날 읽을 책 10권을 주면, 그림과 내용에 빠져 자리에서 일어나지 않았다. 그림 한 장 한 장을 뚫어지게 보고 이 책은 저 책과 같은 작가인 것 같다고 해서 보면 나도 몰랐던 차이점을 찾아내기도 했다. 또한 '그림일까, 사진일까?' 하는 것도 금방 찾아내곤 했다.

"여기는 주인공을 이렇게 그리면 더 좋을텐데 아쉽다."고 하기도 하고, 책의 다음 이야기를 상상하며 스스로 그리고 써 보기도 했다.

  Writing을 즐길 수 있는 다양한 아이디어를 제안하면, 겁 없이 해 보는 아주 창의적인 아이디어가 풍부한 아이였다.

  그렇게 초등과 중등 학습을 마치고 아이 어머니가 오히려 힘들다고 미술을 안 시키려고 하셨는데, 아이의 선택으로 예고에 미술 전공으로 입학하게 되었다.

  모든 아이들은 각자 공부, 음악, 미술, 체육, 법학, 경영, 엔터, 컴퓨터, 유튜버 등 그 아이만의 달란트가 있는것 같다.

  시대가 빠르게 변하고 있다.

  직업도 다양해지고, 사는 방법도 다양해지는 것 같다.

  어떤 것을 선택하든 쉬운 건 없지만, 아이가 잘하고 좋아하는 것이면 그 길이 덜 힘들지 않을까 싶다.

12.
초등부 Class 4

* 외교관 자녀로 잠시 귀국해 2년간 수업 후, 다시 미국으로 가족이 출국.

미술을 전공한 엄마와 외교관인 아빠 사이에서 태어난 초등학교 2학년 아이였다.

'왜 오셨을까?' 궁금했는데, 주재원으로 한국에 몇 년 머물고 다시 출국하게 되어 영어책을 떠나지 않게 하고 싶다고 하셨다.

첫날 들어오자마자 아이는 이렇게 말했다.

"와~ 선생님, 이 책들을 다 어떻게 구입하셨어요? 미국 도서관에서 본 책들이 다 있어요!"

아이는 책을 읽고, 영어로 질문을 하고, 대화하고, Writing을 하며 시간 가는 줄 몰랐다.

책 시리즈가 끝날 때쯤 시리즈 책을 다 읽고 나면 다음 스토리를 스스로 만들어 써 보고 싶다고 하며 그 시간을 너무 즐거워했다.

아이 부모는 아이가 미국으로 다시 돌아가기 전에 한국을 잊지 않고 추억을 만들어 주기 위해 친구들과 많이 어울리게 했다. 한편으로 한국의 유명한 관광지를 견학하며 설명해 주고, 한국어 공부도 신경 쓰시는 것이 보였다.

수업할 때마다 예의와 성품 교육을 소중하게 생각하시는 모습이 놀라왔고, 그런 부모 덕분에 아이는 어떤 아이보다 선하고 예의 바른 아이로 자라는 것 같았다. 나 또한 그 과정에 도움이 되도록 더 많은 관심을 가지고 노력했던 것 같다.

아이 가족이 미국으로 떠난 후, 아이가 영어와 한국어로 시집을 출간했다는 소식을 아이 어머니로부터 전해듣고 너무 기뻤다. 그렇게 어렵고 힘들어하던 골프도 미국에서 드디어 상을 받아 신문에 실렸다는 소식도 들었다.

수줍음 많던 그 아이가 마침내 해냈다는 소식을 듣고, 드디어 저력을 드러냈구나 싶었다.아이가 출간했다는 책을 귀하게 보내주셔서 읽어 보니, 세상을 보는 따뜻한 그 아이의 사랑이 영어로 쓴 글에 그대로 보이는 것 같아서 눈물이 났다.

아이가 떠날 때는 후배들에게 자신이 소장한 책을 함께 보도록 나누고 싶다며 책도 기증하고, 자신이 안 쓰는 소중한 것들은 Flea market을 열어 아파트 앞에서 판매하고 간다는 말에, 오히려 어른인 내가 배워야 할 것 같았다.

이제 많이 컸을 그 아이가 또 어떤 인생 스토리를 쓰고 있을지 궁금하다. 내 연락처가 바뀌며 소식이 끊어져 안타깝지만, 언젠가 또 신문 한켠에 성공 스토리로 올라오지 않을까 기대해 본다.

D.
밖에 나가요

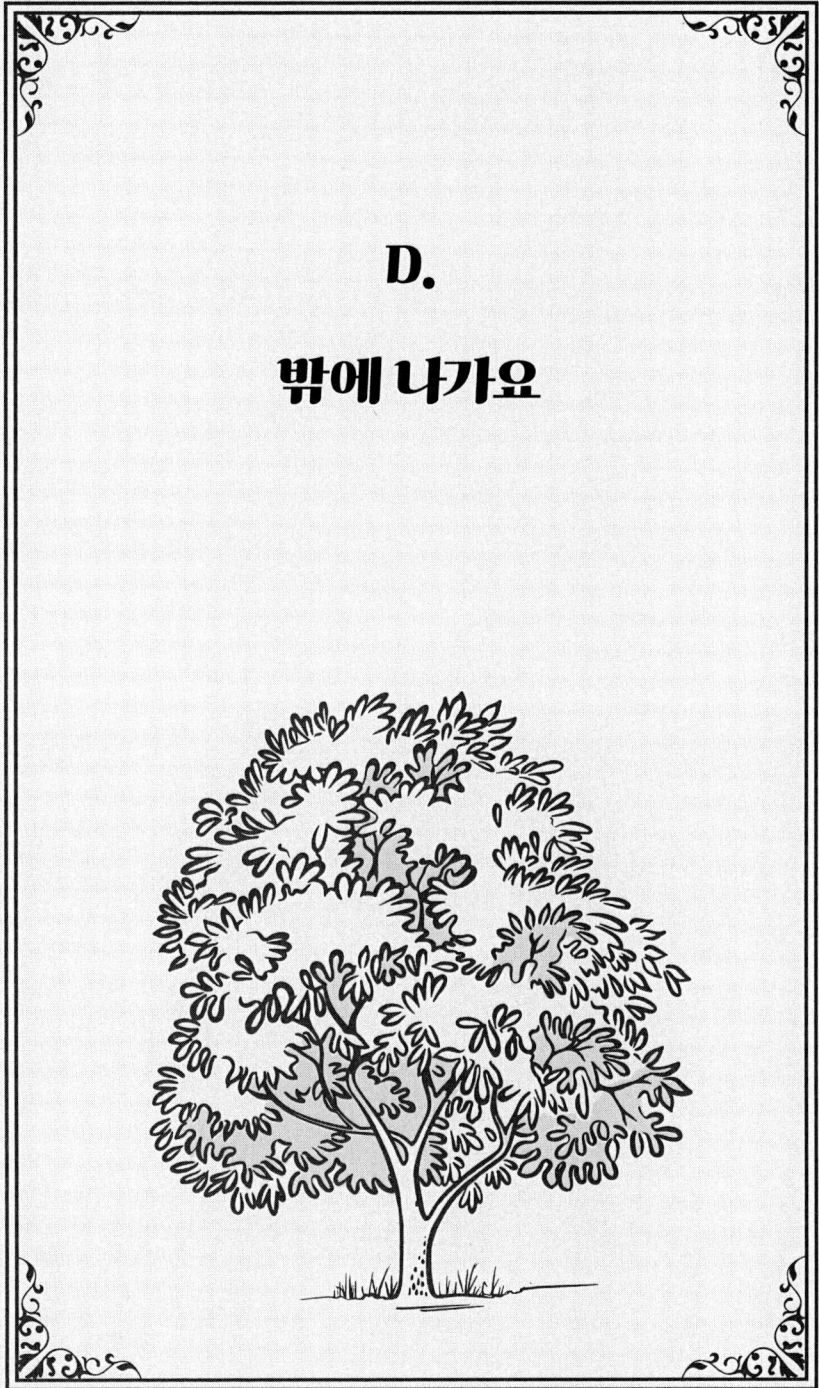

1. 올라가는 버튼 눌러

Never limit yourself. The sky is not the limit-your mind is.
스스로를 제한하지 마라. 하늘이 한계가 아니라 마음이 한계다.

아이랑 쇼핑몰로 놀러 가면 꼭 하게 되는 말들이랍니다.

- 쇼핑 가자.
  Let's go shopping!
- 어디요, 엄마?
  Where, mom?
- 백화점 가는 게 어때?
  How about going to the Department Store?
- 엘리베이터 타자.
  Let's take the elevator.
- 바닥에 앉지 마.
  Don't sit on the floor.
- 올라가는(내려가는) 버튼 눌러라.
  Push the up(down) button.
- 몇 층요?
  Which floor?
- 여기 있어. 곧 돌아올게.

Stay here. I'll be right back.

- 잃어버릴지도 모르니까.
  You might get lost.
- 얼마에요?
  How much is it?
- 좀 내립시다.
  Shall we get off here?
- 좀 비켜 주실래요?
  Excuse me, could you step aside, please?
- 조금 옆으로 움직여 줄래?(공간 확보 원할 때)
  Could you move over?

2. 엄살부리지 마!

Misery loves company.
동병상련.

아플 때, 아이랑 나누게 되는 말이랍니다.

- 어디 아파?　　　　　　What's wrong?
- 몸이 안 좋아요.　　　　 I don't feel well.
- 머리가 아파요.　　　　　I have a headache.
- 목이 아파요.　　　　　　I have a sore-throat.
- 목이 쉬었어요.　　　　　My voice is hoarse.
- 열이 나요.　　　　　　　I have a fever.
- 콧물이 나요.　　　　　　I have a runny nose.
- 코가 막혔어요.　　　　　My nose is stuffed.
- 기침이 나요. / 상대방이 재채기 할 때
  I have a cough. / God bless you.
- 설사가 나요.　　　　　　I have diarrhea.
- 변비 걸렸어요.　　　　　I'm constipated.
- 먹기만 하면 토해요.　　　If I eat, I throw up.

- 눈이 충혈됐어요.　　My eyes are bloodshot.
- 눈이 부었어요.　　My eyelid is swollen.
　　　　　　　　　　My eyelid is puffy.
- 눈이 간질간질해요.　My eyes feel scratchy.
- 이가 흔들려요.　　My tooth is getting very loose.
- 충치가 있어요.　　I have a cavity.
- 뼈가 부러졌어요.　　My bone is broken.
- 데었어요.　　　　I burned myself with boiling water.
- 개에게 팔을 물렸어요.　I was bitten on the arm by a dog.
- 발진이 났어요.　　I have a rash.
- 종종 코피가 나요.　　I often have nosebleeds.
- 가려움을 참을 수가 없어요.　I can't stand this itchiness.
- 열이 내렸어요.　　My fever went down.
- 목구멍에 뼈가 걸렸어요.
  There is a fishbone stuck in my throat.
- 토할 것 같아요.　　I feel like vomiting.
- 목이랑 가슴 좀 진찰해 볼게요.
  Let me check your throat and chest.
- 숨을 크게 들이마셨다 내쉬어 보세요.
  Breathe deeply in and out.
- 언제부터 그랬습니까?　What did it happen?
- 먹은 게 체한 것 같아요.　Something I ate made me sick.
- 설사하나요?　　Do you have diarrhea?
- 감기 걸렸구나.　　I think you have a cold.

D. 밖에 나가요

- 처방전 써드릴게요. I'll write a prescription for you.
- 감기약을 처방해 드릴게요.
  I'll give you a prescription for your cold.
- 주사 맞아야 겠구나. You need to get a shot.
- 약 먹자. Take this medicine.
- 예방 접종해야겠구나. You need to get vaccinated.
- 매 식후에 드세요. Take them after every meal.
- 돌팔이 의사 Quack doctor
- 심장이 뛰는 것을 느껴. I feel my heart beat.
- 입술이 바짝 바짝. My mouth is dry.
- 다리가 후들후들. My leg is weak.
- 다리에 쥐가 났어. My legs have gone to sleep.
- 아야. 근육이 뭉쳤어요. Ouch. My muscles are stiff.
- 어깨가 결려. I have stiff shoulders.
- 허리를 삐었어요. I threw out my back.
- 발목을 삐었어요. I sprained my ankle.
- 팔뼈가 부러졌어요. I fractured my arm.
- 팔뼈를 교정했어요. I got a cast on my arm.
- 신통하게 듣네. It works like a charm.
- 엄마 손은 약손. 예현이 배는 똥배 쑥쑥 내려가라.
  Mom's hands are healing hands.
  Yehyun's belly is potbelly. come out quickly
- 단골 병원 / 주치의 regular clinic / primary doctor

- 나는 단골 병원 주치의에게 진료를 받았어.
  I saw my primary doctor at my regular clinic.

Dialogue

A : I feel sick to my stomach.
B : What did you eat?
A : 위가 아픈 것 같아.
B : 뭐 먹었니?

Key words

- 반창고   band-aid
- 주사   shot
- 연고   ointment
- 찜질   hot pad
- 처방전   prescription
- 소독하다   sterilize
- 깁스   cast
- 혈액형   blood type
- 응급처치실   emergency room
- 청진기   stethoscope
- 가루약   powder
- 안약   eye drops
- 붕대   bandage
- 주사기   needle, syringe
- 침   acupuncture
- 얼음찜질   ice pack
- 목발   crutch
- 소독약   disinfectant
- 수술하다   operate
- 혈압   blood pressure
- 꿰맨 자국   stitch
- 알약   pill
- 시럽   syrup
- 체온계   thermometer

- 해열제　　fever remedy　　· 기침약　　cough syrup
- 약국　　　pharmacy, drugstore
- 면봉　　　cotton swab　　· 부작용　　side effect
- 핀셋　　　tweezer　　　　· 흉터　　　scar
- 벌레 물림　insect bite　　· 수포(물집)　blister
- 두드러기　hives　　　　　· 딱지　　　scab
- 티눈　　　corn
- 땀띠　　　prickly heat, heat rash
- 멍, 몽고반점　　　　　　bruise, Mongolian spot
  일반적인 피부 반점　　　birthmark
- 사마귀　　wart　　　　　· 뽀루지　　rash
- 무좀　　　athlete's feet　· 백선　　　ring worm
- 만병통치약　cure-all
- 일반 약　over-the counter drug
  처방전 약　prescription drug
  항생제　　antibiotics
- 나는 의사에게 항생제를 처방받았어요.
  I was prescribed antibiotics by the doctor.
- 여드름　　pimple　　　　보조개　　　dimple
  주근깨　　freckles
- **symptoms**(증상)
  독감　　　flu　　　　　　수두　　　　chicken pox
  천식　　　asthma　　　　심장병　　　heart disease

장티푸스	typhoid fever	식중독	food poisoning
일사병	sunstroke	대장염	colitis
장염	stomach flu	폐렴	pneumonia
딸꾹질	hiccups	변비	constipation
설사	diarrhea	소화불량	indigestion
화상	burn	중이염	ear infection
꽃가루 알레르기		hay fever, pollinosis	
무좀	athlete's foot		
몽유병	sleepwalking		

- 동네병원

소아과	Pediatrics clinic
한의원	Oriental medicine clinic
내과	Internal medicine clinic
피부과	Dermatology clinic
치과	Dental clinic
안과	Ophthalmology clinic
정형외과	Orthopedic clinic
종합병원	General hospital
응급실	Emergency room(ER)
정신과	Mental health clinic
이비인후과	ENT clinic
산부인과	OB-GYN clinic
단골병원	regular clinic

- 각 진료 과목 의사

	아이에게 쓰는 말	어른이 쓰는 말
소아과 의사	kid's doctor	Pediatrician
한의사	Korean medicine doctor	Korean medicine doctor
내과 의사	doctor	Physician
피부과 의사	skin doctor	Dermatologist
치과 의사	dentist	Dentist
안과 의사	eye doctor	Opthalmologist
정형외과 의사	bone doctor	Orthopedic doctor
정신과 의사	feelings doctor	Psychiatrist
이비인후과 의사	ear, nose and throat doctor	ENT doctor
산부인과 의사	baby doctor for moms	OB-GYN doctor

- 병원에서 하는 대화

  부를 때까지 기다리세요.
  Wait in the waiting room until you're called.

  이마 한 번 짚어 보자.
  Let me feel your forehead.

  들어볼게.
  Let me listen to your heart beat.

  목이랑 가슴 좀 진찰해 볼게.
  Let me check your throat and chest.

  숨을 크게 들이마셨다 내쉬어 보세요.
  Breathe deeply in and out.

아, 해봐.	Say ah~
언제 부터였어?	When did your pain start?
어제부터.	Since yesterday.
감기 걸렸구나.	You have a cold.
처방전 써드릴게요.	I'll write a prescription for you.
주사 맞아야겠구나.	You need to get a shot.
걱정 마. 조금 따끔할 거야.	Don't worry. It just a little sting.
아야, 아파요.	Ouch. That hurts.
엄살부리지 마.	Don't exaggerate.
잘했다. 다 컸네.	Good job. You're so grown up.
매 식후에 드세요.	Take them after every meal.
약은 너무 써서 싫어.	The medicine is so bitter.

하루에 세 번 식후에 먹어.
Take the medicine three times, after every meal.

약 먹고 나니 졸려.	The medicine made me drowsy.
약 먹고 나니 좋아졌어.	After taking the medicine, I felt better.
열이 내렸어요.	My fever went down.
속이 메스꺼워.	I feel nauseous.
꾀병이지?	Are you faking it?
몸살 났어요.	I'm under the weather.

목과 어깨가 뻣뻣해요(오래 앉아 있거나 자세가 안 좋을 때).
My neck and shoulders are stiff.

근육이 뻣뻣하고 아파요(운동 후 근육통에).
My muscle feels tight and sore.

D. 밖에 나가요

근육이 당겨요(근육을 다쳤을 때. 근육을 삐끗했어요).
I pulled a muscle.

나는 (배멀미 / 차멀미 / 비행기멀미 / 버스멀미)가 나요.
I feel sea-sick / car-sick / air-sick / bus-sick

Dialogue

M : How was school?

K : It was terrible.

M : What happened?

K : I sprained my ankle while. I was playing soccer.

M : Oh no! You should have been more careful.

K : I won't be able to play soccer for a while.

M : 학교 어땠어?

K : 엉망이었어요.

M : 무슨 일 있었어?

K : 발목을 삐었어요. 축구하다가.

M : 저런, 조심하지 않고.

K : 얼마 동안 축구 못할 거예요.

3. 햄버거 먹으러 가자

This is on me.
내가 살게.

가끔 아이들이랑 가면 꼭 필요한 표현.

- 뭐 먹을래?
  What would you like to have?
- 결정하게 잠깐만 기다려주세요.
  Give me a minute to decide what I want.
- 그러렴.
  Sure, take your time.
- 나는 불고기 버거 세트 메뉴 할래요.
  I'd like to have a bulgogi hamburger combo meal.
- 다른 건 안 필요하신가요?
  Anything else?
- 여기서 드실 건가요? 포장하실 건가요?
  For here or to go?
- 프렌치프라이 2인분 주세요.
  Please give me two orders of french fries.
- 1만2천 원 되겠습니다.

That will be 12,000 won.

- 지금 곧 나옵니다.
  Coming right up.

- 지금 준비 중입니다.
  It's on the way.

- 냅킨 좀 가져올래?
  Can you bring me a napkin?

- 셔츠에 다 튀었잖아!
  You got it all over your shirt!

- 감자튀김에 케첩 찍어 먹어.
  Dip your fries in the ketchup.

- 내가 살게.
  This is on me.

- 이 음료수는 서비스입니다.
  This drink is on the house.

- 나 여기 단골이야.
  I'm a regular here.

4. 배에서 꼬르륵 소리가 나요

Hunger is the best sauce.
시장이 반찬.

음식하기 싫은 날, 아이랑 이런 대화는 어떨까요?

- 저녁식사에 계획 있어요?　　　Any plans for dinner?
- 집에서 저녁 먹을까요, 아니면 나가서 먹을까요?
　　　　　　　　　　　　　　Dine in or carry out?
- 오늘 밤엔 외식해요.　　　　　Let's eat out tonight.
- 전화로 저녁 시켜 먹을까?　　　How about calling out for dinner?
- 저녁 시켜 먹어야겠다.　　　　Let's call out for dinner.
- 점심에 먹던 걸로 때우자.　　　Let's have the leftovers from lunch.
- 상관없어요. 마음대로 하세요.　I don't mind. It's up to you.
- 배고프니? 겨우 5시인데.　　　Are you hungry? It's only 5 p.m
- 배에서 소리가 나요.　　　　　My stomach is growling.
- 난 뭐든 간절히 먹고 싶어요.　I'm dying for some.

5. 피자 먹고 싶은 사람

Life is not all pizza and sunshine.
인생이 항상 순조롭고 즐겁지만은 않다.

- 피자 먹고 싶은 사람   Who's craving pizza?
- 저요.   Me.
- 주문하자.   Let's order pizza.
- 크기는?   What size would you like?
- 엑스트라라지로.   I want an extra-large.
- 피자에 토핑을 어떻게 할까?
  What toppings would you like on your pizza?
- 나는 베이컨 피자로 할래요.   I'll take the bacon pizza.
- 주소는?   What's your address?
- 더 필요한 건?   Anything else?
- 없어요. 그것만 주세요.   No, just that, please.
- 감사합니다. 피자를 곧 배달해 드릴게요.
  Thank you. Your pizza will be delivered soon.

6. 사진이 흐릿해요

Say cheese!
웃으세요!

- 사진 찍어 주세요.   Could you take our picture, please?
- 다시 찍어 주세요.   One more time, please.
- 다시 찍을게.   Let me take it again.
- 각도가 마음에 안 들어.   I don't like this angle.
- 포즈를 취해 줘.   Pose for a picture.
- 네 위치로 가.   Go back to your position.
- 네 손이 약간 흔들렸어.   Your hands were a little shaky.
- 사진이 흐릿해.   The picture is blurry.
- 움직이지 마.   Don't move.
- 카메라 보세요.   Look at the camera.
- 사진이 멋지다.   The picture is great.
- 얼짱   good-looking
- 이 사진이 실물보다 잘 나왔군요. This picture flatters you.
- 실제 모습이 더 나아요.   You look nicer in person.
- 몸짱인 남자   Beefcake

Dialogue

L.B : Are these your vacation pictures?

B.B : Yes, they are.

L.B : Hey, this picture flatters you.

B.B : Thanks, I took it on the mountain.

L.B : Who's this standing beside you?

B.B : Oh, that's John. He is the best singer in my class.

L.B : 이거 캠프 때 찍은 사진이야?

B.B : 응.

L.B : 야, 이 사진은 실물보다 잘 나왔네.

B.B : 고마워, 산에서 찍은 거야.

L.B : 형아, 옆에 서 있는 사람은 누구야?

B.B : 아, 존이야. 그는 우리 반에서 최고 가수야.

이 사진이 실물보다 잘 나왔군요.

This picture flatters you.

You look nicer in this picture.

실제모습이 더 나아요.

You look nicer in person.

7. 형광펜 사러 가요

Don't be sharp.
너무 날카롭게 굴지마.

문방구는 모두에게 즐거운 세상이죠? 영어로 해볼까요?

- 어디 가니?
  Where are you headed?
- 문방구에.
  I'm going to the stationery store.
- 왜?
  What for?
- 형광펜, 사인펜 사러.
  To buy highlighters and felt-tip-pens.
- 아! 나도 생각났는데, 나도 살게 있어.
  Ah! That reminds me. I need something at the stationery store, too.
- 같이 갈래?
  Want to come along?
- 찾을 수가 없어요.
  I can't find it.

D. 밖에 나가요

- 거기에 좀 있을 텐데.
  There should be some there.
- 벌써 확인해 봤는데 없어요.
  I already checked there but there isn't any.
- 뒤쪽 통로에 있어.
  In the back aisle.
- 총 2만 원입니다.
  Your total comes to 20,000 won.
- 하든지 말든지 결정해.
  Take it or leave it.
- 뭔가 생각났어. / 감동의 의미일 때 가슴을 치며 쓸 수도
  Something hits me.

Stationery

샤프	mechanical pencil
색연필	colored pencil
연필깎이	pencil sharpener
호치키스	stapler
호치키스 심	staples
자	ruler
가위	scissors
계산기	calculator
서류철	folder
형광펜	highlighter
사인펜	felt-tip-pen
수정펜	white-out
고무 밴드	rubber band
구멍 내는 것	hole puncher
3공 링바인더	Three-ring binder
다이어리	planner
책갈피	book mark
압정	thump tack
교복	school uniform
운동복	gym uniform

8. 난 음치에요

You are singing off-key.
음정이 틀려.

- 노래방 가볼까?
  Shall we go to No-Rae Bang?
- 방에 기계가 있어.
  There is a machine in the room.
- 먼저 노래 키를 조정해.
  First adjust the song's key.
- 노래책에서 노래를 선곡해.
  Choose a song from the songbook.
- TV 화면 가사를 따라해.
  Follow the lyrics of the song displayed on the TV screen.
- 음정이 틀리잖아.
  You're singing off-key.
- 나는 음치라서 노래할 때 항상 음정을 못 맞춰.
  I'm tone deaf so I can't carry a tune.
- 그만해.   **Cut it out.**
- 마이크 넘겨.   **Pass me the mike.**
- 동생에게 기회 한 번 더 줘라.

Give her another chance.

- 너 목소리가 갔다. Your voice is gone.
- 말도 거의 못해. You can barely talk.
- 책 한 번 쭉 훑어볼게.
  Let me look through the song book.
- 아는 노래가 하나도 없네.
  I can't find any songs that I know.
- 누가 첫 곡 부를래?
  Who's going to sing the first song?
- 나~ 음악을 잘 알아. I have a good ear for music.
- 내가 해볼게요. I'll give it a try.
- 내가 먼저 해도 되는데. I can go first.
- 어차피 할 거 먼저 할래요. I'll get this over with first.
- 저 노래 정말 못해요. I can't carry a tune.
- 내가 저 노래 부르려고 했는데.
  I was going to sing that song.
- 그녀는 음성이 좋아 She has a great voice.
- 잘해봐. Break a leg. / Go for it.
- 소리가 크게 안 나와. The sound isn't loud enough.
- 모니터는 나오는데, 마이크가 안 돼.
  The TV is working ,but the mike isn't.
- 한번 해봐 Go for it. / Try it.
- 다음에 할게요. I'll pass on that. / I'll try next time.
- 너의 실력을 발휘해 봐. Do your stuff.

- 목이 쉬었어요.
  There's a frog in my throat./I have a frog in a throat.
- 음높이가 맞지 않게 노래 부르고 있구나.
  You are singing off key.
- 난 음치에요.
  I'm tone- deaf.   I can't carry a tune. / I'm a poor singer.

Dialogue

M : Let's go singing, shall we?

K : Singing? Where?

M : At a No-lae-bang. It'll be fun.

K : I'm sorry, but I refuse. I'm tone-deaf.

M : That's why we go there. A No-lae-bang is a place where people can practice singing.

K : Well, in that case, okay.

엄마 : 노래하러 가자.

아이 : 노래요? 어디요?

엄마 : 노래방에. 재미있을 거야.

아이 : 미안해요 안 갈래요. 난 음치에요.

엄마 : 그러니까 가야지. 노래방은 노래 연습하는 곳이야.

아이 : 그럼, 좋아요.

9. 가슴이 찡했어요

I had a lump in my throat.
가슴이 뭉클했어요.

- 오늘 저녁 영화 한 편 볼까?
  How about watchting a movie tonight?
- 좋아요.
  Sounds great.
- 난 만화영화가 좋아
  I like cartoons.
- Golden은 아직 영화로 출시되지 않았어.
  The Golden is not out on movie yet.
- "그럼 'Inside out'은 어때?"
  How about 'Inside out'?
- 네가 안 좋아하더라도 그건 꼭 봐야 돼.
  Even if you don't like it,you have to see it.
- 액션이 시시해.
  The action is lame.
- 줄거리가 뻔해요.
  The plot is so predictable.

- 여주인공, 남주인공

  heroine, hero.

- 빨리 돌리지 마.

  Don't fast-forward the movie.

- 감아 봐요.

  Rewind it.

- 볼륨 좀 높여.

  Turn up the volume.

- 자막 좀 나오게 해주세요.

  Put on the subtitles.

- 기계 제대로 설치해 놓은 거니?

  Did you set up the machine correctly?

- 볼륨 좀 낮춰.

  Turn down the volume.

- 가슴이 뭉클했어요.

  I had a lump in my throat.

- 주연

  lead actor / lead actress

  조연

  supporting actor

Dialogue

M : How about renting a movie tonight?

K : That's a good idea.

M : Which movie do you want to rent?

K : How about 'Sister Act'?

M : Who is starring in the film?

K : Whoopi Goldberg is starring in the film.

M : Who's in it?

K : I don't know but I like the songs.

엄마 : 오늘밤 영화 하나 빌려 볼까?

아이 : 좋은 생각이에요.

엄마 : 어느 영화를 빌릴까?

아이 : '시스터 액트'는 어때요?

엄마 : 영화 주연이 누구야?

아이 : 우피 골디버그가 영화 주연이에요.

엄마 : 누가 출연했어?

아이 : 몰라요 그렇지만, 특히 난 그 노래가 좋아요.

10. 깎아 주세요

Penny wise, pound foolish.
작은 일에 집착, 큰일엔 어리석다는 말.

- 전부 얼마에요. How much is that all?
- 전부 12,000원이에요. It's 12000 won altogether.
- 여기 20,000원 이에요. Here is 20,000won.
- 여기 거스름돈이에요. Here is your change.
- 비닐에 넣어 주세요. Put it in a plastic bag for me.
- 종이봉지에 넣어 주세요. Put it in a paper bag for me.
- 고맙습니다. 또 오세요. Thank you. Come again, please.
- 충동구매 Impulse shopping
- 비싸다 / 싸다 / 저렴하다 expensive / cheap / reasonable
- 깎아 주세요. Give me a discount
- 옷 사는데 많은 돈을 낭비했어.
  I wasted a lot of money on clothes.
- 분수 좀 알아라. Be real / Get real.
- 낭비가 심하네. What a spender!
- 공짜로 줄게. I'll give it to you for free.

- 3천 원에 3개 줄게.
  I'll give you three for three thousand.
- 환불 안 돼요.　　　　　　　　No refund.
- 신어 봐도 될까요?　　　　　　May I try these on?
- 잔돈은 가지세요.　　　　　　 Keep the change.
- 이거 가져도 좋아.　　　　　　You may take this.
- 정찰제　　　　　　　　　　　Fixed price.
- 다 팔렸어요.　　　　　　　　 It was sold out.
- 질질 끌지 말고 결정해.
  Stop dragging your feet and decide.
- 그냥 구경합니다.　　　　　　 I'm just browsing.
- 할인율이 얼마인가요?　　　　 What's the discount rate?
- 지금 특별 세일 중입니다.　　　It's on special sale now.
- 잔돈으로 바꿔 주실 수 있나요?　Can you break this bill?
- 나는 충동구매를 잘해.　　　　I'm an impulsive shopper.
- 돈이 하나도 없어.　　　　　　I'm broke.
- 내가 살게.　　　　　　　　　This is on me.
- 둘 중에 아무거나 좋아.　　　　Either will do.
- 또 들러주세요.　　　　　　　 Please stop by again.
- 완전 바가지잖아!　　　　　　 What a rip-off!
- 가격표　　　　　　　　　　　price tag

D. 밖에 나가요

11. 백억

Money = my one
내 것만 생각하라. 늘 남의 부유함에 속상해 말고.

- 만   ten thousand
- 십만   one hundred thousand
- 백만   one million
- 천만   ten million
- 1억   one hundred million
- 십억   one billion
- 백억   ten billion
- 1,000억   one hundred billion
- 1조   one trillion
- 십조   ten trillion
- 백조   one hundred trillion
- 천조   one hundred quadrillion
- 10분의 7   seven tenth
- 50부터 거꾸로 세어 보세요.   Count down from 50
- 난 숫자에 약해.   I'm not good at numbers.

- 숫자엔 머리가 잘 돌아가. I have brains for figures.
- 아이 양육비 child support
- 판매를 한다는 뜻 For sale
  세일(가격을 할인)한다는 뜻 On sale

미국 돈 배워 볼까요?

종류	가치	인물	색깔
penny	1cent	에이브러햄 링컨	구리색
nickel	5cent	토마스 제퍼슨	은색
dime	10cent	프랭클린 루즈벨트	은색
quarter	25cent	조지 워싱턴	은색
half dollar	50cent	존 에프 케네디	은색
dollar	100cent	조지 워싱턴	흰 바탕에 녹색

D. 밖에 나가요

Dialogue

K : Wow! Mom, look at that doll in the window.

M : Yeah, it looks nice. But I wonder how much it would be.
This place is quite expensive.
Let me see the price tag. Oh, my goodness!
100 thousand won. What a rip-off!
Who would want to spend that much on a kid's doll?

K : Mom. But I want it. PLEASE!

M : Hold it down! Let just leave. This place is a little too rich for us.

K : I can't find anything better than that.

K : 우와! 엄마 창안에 인형 보세요.

M : 그래, 정말 멋있다.
하지만 가격이 얼마나 할지 궁금한 걸.
이곳은 꽤 비싼 곳이거든.
가격표를 볼게. 이런 세상에!
10만 원이야. 완전히 바가지잖아!
누가 아이 인형 사는데 그런 돈을 쓰냐?

K : 엄마 그래도 사고 싶어요.

M : 소리 낮춰! 그냥 가자.
이곳은 우리 같은 사람한테는 너무 비싸다고.

K : 난 저 인형보다 더 나은 건 못 찾겠는데.

12. 롤러코스터 타러 갈까?

Too many cooks spoil the broth.
사공이 많으면 배가 산으로 간다.

- 자유이용권을 사요.
  Let's buy a pass for all the rides.
- 몇 개 탈 수 있는 걸로 사요.
  Let's just buy a pass for a few rides.
- 우와 저 탈 것들 좀 보세요.
  Wow, look at all the rides.
- 먼저 뭐 타고 싶니?
  Which ride do you want to go on first?
- 무서운 놀이기구는 안 타고 싶어요.
  I don't want to go on any scary rides.
- 토할 것 같아요.
  I feel like throwing up.
- 대신 저거 탈래요.
  I want to go on that ride instead.
- 길 잃어버리지 마.
  Don't get lost.

- 서로 붙어 다녀.
  Stay close together.
- 너무 멀리 가지 마.
  Don't wander off.
- 1시간 후에 여기서 만나자.
  Let's meet here in one hour.
- 무서워 내내 눈을 꼭 감았어요.
  I kept my eyes shut for the whole ride.
- 저 놀이기구 진짜 재미있어요.
  That ride is awesome. (incredible, amazing, cool)
- 쉬면서 좀 먹자.
  Let's take a break and get something to eat.
- 오늘 재미있었니?
  Was it fun today?
- 오늘 하루를 여기서 다 보냈네.
  We spent all day at the amusement park.
- 다음에 또 와요.
  Let's come here again.
- 같이 못가니까 속상해.
  It's shame that you can't join us.
- 계획이 수포로 돌아갔어.
  My plans went up in smoke.
- 난 높은 곳에서 현기증이 나요.
  I suffer from vertigo.
- 저는 고소공포증이 있어요.
  I have acrophobia.

- 나는 꼭대기 층에 살아.
  I live on the tippy-top floor.(어린이나 귀엽게 강조하는 말투로 가능)
  I live on the top floor.

Dialogue

M : What are you doing next weekend?

K : Nothing much.

M : Would you like to go to an amusement park and go on some roller coasters?

K : No, I'm afraid of heights.

M : But it's so thrilling!

K : You go without me. I'll just stay home and watch TV.

M : 다음 주말에 뭐할래?

K : 별다른 것 없어요.

M : 롤러코스터 타러 갈까?

K : 아뇨, 난 높은 것이 무서워요.

M : 하지만 스릴 있잖아.

K : 혼자 가세요. 저는 그냥 집에서 TV 볼게요.

13. 주의하세요

Kill two birds with one stone.
꿩 먹고 알 먹고.

- 먹이 주지 마.
  Don't feed the animals.
- 우리에 물건 던지지 마.
  Don't throw things into the animal cages.
- 막대기로 그걸 찌르지 마.
  Don't poke sticks at it.
- 유리를 세게 치지 마세요.
  Don't pound on the glass.
- 사진 찍을 때 플래시를 꺼 주세요.
  No flash photography.
- 음식물 반입 금지
  No food or drinks are allowed in this area.
- 뛰어다니지 마.
  No running around.
- 야생동물 근처에 가지 마세요.
  Don't get too close to wild animals.

- 줄 서.
  Line up. Stay in line.
- 동물들에게 소리치지 마.
  Don't yell at them.
- 이제부터 조용히 해야 해.
  You have to be quiet here.
- 폭신한, 털이 보풀한, 매끄러운, 말랑한, 부드러운
  fluffy, fuzzy, smooth, squishy, soft.
- 무조건 모방
  Monkey see, monkey do.

Dialogue

K : wah wah~ I lost my mom. I have looked everywhere but can't find her. Please announce it.

E : Sure, How smart. What is your name?

K : ~~

E : Okay. We'll broadcast it right away. Hang on a second and don't cry any more.

K : 으앙, 엄마를 잃어버렸어요. 아무리 찾아봐도 없어요. 방송해 주세요.

E : 그럼. 똑똑하구나. 이름이 뭐지?

K : ~~

E : 알겠어. 바로 방송할게. 잠시 기다려 더 이상 울지 말고.

14. 그 책 빌릴 수 있나요?

Reading is an exercise in empathy.
책은 공감을 연습하는 곳이다.

- 어떤 책을 찾고 있어요.
  I'm looking for a book.
- 작가의 색인을 이용할 수 있어요.
  You can use the author's index.
- 아니면 제목으로 찾을 수 있어요.
  Or you can search by the title.
- 대출이 되었습니다.
  It's been checked out.
- 일주일간 대출할 수 있어요.
  You can have it for one week.
- 열람표를 작성해 주세요.
  Fill out a call slip.
- 얼마 동안 대출할 수 있나요?
  How long can I check out this book?
- 늦게 반납하면 하루 1달러씩 벌금을 내셔야 합니다.
  If you turn it late, you have to pay one dollar a day.

- 다른 사람이 예약해 둔 책이네요.
  It has been reserved by another user.
- 만기일이 2월 1일이에요.
  It's due on February 1st.
- 대출 기한을 연장할 수 있어요.
  You can renew it.

Dialogue

A : Excuse me, I can't find this book.

B : It's been checked out. It's due on June 3rd.

A : We'll let you know as soon as the book is returned.

A : 실례지만 이 책을 찾을 수 없어요.

B : 그것은 대출이 되었고, 만기일이 6월 3일입니다.

A : 그 책이 반환되는 즉시 당신께 알려 줄게요.

15. 얼마나 더 가야 되요?

To travel is to live. - *Hans Christian Andersen*
여행하는 것은 살아가는 것이다. - 안데르센

- 엄마, 저 학교에 차로 태워다 주실 수 있어요?
  Mom, can you give me a ride to school?

- 미안, 엄마가 지금 꽤 바쁘구나.
  I'm sorry but I'm quite busy at the moment.

- 알았어요.   All right.
- 다 와 가나요?   Mom, are we almost there?
- 다 와 가요.   We are almost there.
- 반쯤 왔어요.   We're about halfway there.
- 반쯤 지나왔어.   We've passed about halfway.
- 다 왔어요.   Here we are.
- 얼마나 더 가야 되요? How much further to go?
- 그렇게 멀어요?   Is it really that far?
- 어디 내려서 뭐 좀 먹을까?
  Why don't we stop off somewhere for a bite?
- 정말 긴 여행이야.   It's a long journey!
- 얼마나 더 가야 되요? How much further to go?

- 다리도 좀 뻗고 싶어요.　　I want to stretch my legs a bit.
- 반쯤 지나왔습니다.　　We've passed about halfway.
- 그의 차가 정면충돌했어요.　He was in a head-on collision.
- 그의 차는 추돌 당했어요.　He got rear-ended.
- 그의 차 측면이 들이받혔어요.　　He was hit broadside.

Dialogue

Kid : Mom, are we almost there?

M : We're about halfway there.

Kid : Wow, is it really that far?

M : Yes, why don't we stop off somewhere for a bite?

Kid : Good idea. I'd like to go to the bathroom.

M : Here we are. What would you like to have?

Kid : walnut, squid and ice cream cone.

Kid : 엄마 다 와 가요?

M : 반쯤 왔어.

Kid : 와 정말 그렇게 먼가요?

M : 그래, 어디 내려서 뭐 좀 먹을까?

Kid : 좋은 생각이에요. 화장실에 가고 싶어요.

M : 다 왔다. 뭐 먹을래?

Kid : 호두, 오징어 그리고 아이스크림

16. 보글보글

Hungers can not choose.
찬밥 더운밥 가리랴.

보글보글

보글보글 짝짝 지글지글 짝짝

보글짝 지글짝 보글지글 짝짝

boiling boiling clap clap

sizzling sizzling clap clap

boiling clap sizzling clap

boiling sizzling clap clap

- 엄마, 밥 언제 먹죠?   Mom, when do we eat?
- 배고파 죽겠어요.   I'm starving to death.
- 배에서 꼬르륵 소리가 나요.   My stomach is growling
- 식욕이 없어요.   I have a poor appetite.
- 와서 먹어.   Come and get it.
- 상 차리는 것 도와줄래?   Can you help me set the table?
- 접시 이가 나갔어요.   There is a chip in this plate.

- 금이 갔어요. It is cracked.
- 깨졌어요. It was broken.
- 어디 놔야 되죠? Where should I put the dish?
- 나 깡통 딸 수 있어요. I can can a can.
- 엄마는 훌륭한 요리사야. You are a good cook.
- 달걀을 어떻게 해줄까? How would you like your eggs?
- 중간 불에 멸치 볶아 주세요.
  Stir-fry the anchovies over medium heat.
- 생선을 뒤집어야겠어.
  I need to flip the fish over!
- 핫도그를 전자레인지에 데워 주세요.
  Microwave a few hot dogs.
- 한쪽, 양쪽, 스크램블, 반숙, 완숙?
  sunny-side up, over easy, scrambled, soft boiled, hard boiled
- 계란 노른자 yolk
  흰자 white
  껍질 shell
- 재료를 섞어라. Mix the ingredients.
- 약한 불에 한 시간 끓여라 Simmer for 1 hour.
- 도마가 너무 작아. The cutting board is too small.
- 칼이 무디네. The knife is dull.
- 잘 들게 해야겠다. It needs to be sharpened.
- 생선에 반죽옷 입히자. Let's batter the fish.
- 미지근해요. It is lukewarm.

D. 밖에 나가요

- 맛 한 번 보세요. Taste this.
- 난 땅콩 알레르기가 있어. I'm allergic to peanut.
- 군침이 도는군요.
  My mouth is watering.
- 둘이 먹다 하나 죽어도 모를 정도로 맛있어.
  This food is delicious enough to make a cat speak.
- 양파를 깔 때 눈이 따가워 눈물이 났어요.
  My eyes watered when I peeled the onions.

How to prepare

헹구다	rinse	잘게 썰다	chop
얇게 자르다	slice	깍뚝썰기하다	dice(cube)
저미다	mince(Br E), grind(AmE)		
강판에 갈다	grate	껍질을 벗기다.	peel
찢다	shred		

cookery

퓨레 puree
(food that is boiled or crushed until it is soft mass that is almost liquid)

절이다	marinate
튀기다	fry
석쇠로 굽다	grill
오븐 등의 열로 굽다	bake

직접 불에 쬐어 굽다	broil
굽다(빵)	toast
기름에 살짝 튀기다 (cook something quickly in a little hot oil or fat)	saute
약한 불에 끓이다.	simmer
양념장을 칠하다.	baste
반죽 옷을 입히다.	batter
세게 휘젓다.	beat
섞다.	blend, mix
짜다	squeeze
반죽하다	knead
졸이다(약한 불에 오래 끓여)	reduce
양념하다 간을 맞추다	season
찌다	steam

Cookware

냄비	pot	냄비뚜껑	lid
팬	pan	뒤집게 주걱	spatula
국자	ladle	주전자	kettle
물주전자	jug	티스푼	teaspoon
도마	cutting board	테이블스푼	table spoon
밀대	rolling pin	볼	bowl
계량컵	measuring cup	집게	tongs

체	sieve	오븐장갑	oven mitts
거품기	whisk	강판	grater
깡통따개	can opener	코르크 마개뽑이	corkscrew
밥솥	rice cooker	냉장고	refrigerator
식기세척기	dishwasher	믹서	electric grinder
레몬즙짜개	lemon squeezer	압력솥	pressure cooker
냄비받침	hot pad	냄비장갑	hot glove
저울	scale	이쑤시개	toothpick

Seasoning

간장	soy sauce	빵가루	bread crumbs
청국장	fermented soybeans	설탕	sugar
된장	soybean paste	소금	salt
고추장	hot pepper paste	고춧가루	hot pepper
겨자	mustard	후춧가루	black pepper
밀가루	flour	생강	ginger powder
청주	sake	계피	cinnamon
게맛살	crab-meat blend	식초	vinegar
통조림	canned food		

vegetables

양상추	lettuce	우엉	burdock
오이	cucumber	연근	lotus root
양배추	cabbage	콩나물	bean sprout
당근	carrot	숙주나물	green bean sprout
양파	onion	강낭콩	string bean
시금치	spinach	가지	eggplant
무	radish	고사리	bracken
피망	green pepper	마	yam
늙은 호박	pumpkin	버섯	mushroom
서양 호박	zucchini	토란	taro
호박	squash	부추	garlic chives
감자	potato	대파	green onion
고구마	sweet potato	쪽파	scallion
실파	chives		

Grains and nuts

팥	red beans
보리	barley
귀리	oats
밀	wheat
밤	chestnut

fruit

석류	pomegranate
금귤	kumquat
감	persimmon
무화과	fig
건포도	raisin

호두	walnut	자두	plum
배	pear	복숭아	peach
포도	grape	버찌	black cherry
귤	tangerine	살구	apricot
곶감	dried persimmon	홍시	mellow persimmon

seaweed

김	laver	다시마	kelp
파래	green laver		

fish

장어	eel	미꾸라지	mudfish / butterfish
가자미	flounder	고등어	mackerel
조기	yellow corbina	정어리	sardine
꽁치	saury	갈치	hair tail fish
참치	tuna	송어	trout
숭어	mullet	연어	salmon
잉어	carp	대구	cod fish
홍합	mussel	대합	clam
새우	shrimp	문어	octopus
가리비	scallop	전복	sea ear, abalone
오징어	squid	게	crab

굴	oyster	멍게	sea squirt
해산물	sea food	오징어	squid, cuttle fish
낙지	small octopus	연어알	salmon roe(eggs)
키조개	razor clam	멸치	anchovies

Dialogue

M : Oh, my god! I forgot the soup. David, please stir the soup in the kitchen.

K : I'm busy changing the baby's diaper. I have too many irons in the fire everyday!

M : Watch out you might get burned.

K : Don't worry, it's as easy as pie, mom.

M : 오 이런! 스프를 잊고 있었네. 데이빗, 부엌에 스프 좀 저어 줘.

K : 난 아기 기저귀 가느라 바쁘거든. 매일 눈코 뜰 새 없이 바쁘네.

M : 데지 않게 조심해.

K : 걱정 마세요. 식은 죽 먹기에요.

Tea

대추차	jujube tea	녹차	green tea
오미자차	berry tea	홍차	black tea
식혜	rice punch	쌍화차	herb tonic tea
수정과	cinnamon punch	숭늉	burnt-rice tea

D. 밖에 나가요

유자차	citron tea	홍삼차	red ginseng tea

Liquor

동동주	fermented rice wine
인삼주	ginseng liquor
막걸리	unstrained rice wine
산사춘	rice wine
소주	vodka-like drink

food

볶음밥	fried rice
자장면	noodles in black bean sauce
탕수육	sweet and sour pork
초밥	raw fish on rice
전복죽	rice porridge with abalone(ear shell)
꽃게찜	steamed blue crab
어묵	processed seafood cakes in broth
물김치	cold kimchi soup
깍두기	cubed radish kimchi
불고기	barbecued beef slices and lettuce wrap
닭갈비	pan-fried chicken
닭꼬치	spicy grilled chicken on skewers

족발	steamed pork hocks
삼겹살	barbecued bacon-type pork
잡채	stir-fried noodles and vegetables
칼국수	thick handmade noodles in broth
콩국수	noodles in cold soy milk soup
물냉면	buckwheat noodles in cold broth
돌솥밥	hot pot rice
쌈밥	assorted ingredients with rice and wraps
장어구이	grilled eel
광어회	raw halibut
감자탕	meaty bones and potato soup
만두국	soup with meat filled dumplings
부대찌개	ham and scraps stew
순두부	spicy uncurdled tofu stew
도토리묵	acorn jelly
샤브샤브	DIY beef and vegetable casserole
수제비	dough flakes in shellfish broth

Dialogue

M : How's the stew?

K : It's delicious. You really outdid yourself.

M : Don't put me on.

K : I'm serious, This is really good.

M : Do you really think so?

K : Yes, I really mean it. I can't get enough of it myself.

엄마 : 찌개 맛 어때?

아이 : 맛있어요. 평소보다 더 맛있어요.

엄마 : 비행기 태우지 마.

아이 : 정말이에요. 진짜 맛있어요.

엄마 : 정말 그렇게 생각하니?

아이 : 그럼, 정말이라니까요. 난 아무리 먹어도 물리지가 않아요.

비행기 태우지 마.	Don't put me on.
	Don't flatter me.
	You're flattering me.
우쭐대지 마	Don't flatter yourself.

* 한국: 보양탕
* 미국 : 칠면조
* 프랑스: 달팽이 요리
* 멕시코: 비둘기 요리

E.

놀아요

1. 비눗방울 날려요

Don't burst my bubble.
내 비눗방울 터뜨리지 마.

- 비눗방울 놀이 하자.　　Let's play with the bubbles.
- 난다.　　　　　　　　They float. / It floats.
- 봐 날아간다.　　　　　Look at them go!
- 와 크다　　　　　　　Wow it's so big!
- 저것은 정말 크다.　　　That one is so big.
- 터졌다.　　　　　　　It popped.
- 잡았다.　　　　　　　I got it.
- 날려 보자.　　　　　　Let the bubble fly away.

2. 올림머리 하고 싶어요

Fashion is a way to say who you are without having to speak.
- Rachel Zoe
패션은 말을 하지 않고도 자신을 표현하는 방법이다.

- 인형놀이 하자.   Let's play with dolls.
- 목욕시켜 주자.   Let's give the doll a bath.
- 업어 주자.   Let's give her a piggyback ride.
- 인형 재우자.   Let's put the doll to bed.
- 머리 묶어 주자.   Let's tie back the doll's hair.
- 옷 입혀 주자.   Let's dress the doll.
- 안아 주자.   Let's hug the doll.
- 밥 먹이자.   Let's feed the doll.
- 하나로.   In a ponytail
- 하나로 땋아.   In one braid
- 둘로 땋아.   In two braids
- 하나로 방울처럼   In a bun
- 두 개로 방울처럼   In two buns
- 머리숱이 많아.   It has thick hair.
- 올림머리 하고 싶어.   I'd like to wear my hair up.

- 애교머리
  bangs
- 머리를 어떻게 잘라드릴까요?
  How would you like your hair cut?
- 앞머리를 잘라 주세요.
  Shorten the bangs.
- 옆머리를 쳐 주세요.
  Thin out the side.
- 끝에 약간만 잘라 주세요.
  Trim a little bit off the ends.
- 층지게 잘라 주세요.
  Layer the hair.
- 옆을 다듬고 뒤는 조금씩 작게 쳐 주세요.
  Trim the sides and taper it in the back.
- 특이하다
  It's so unique.

3. 와르르

Home is the nicest word there is. - Laura Ingalls Wilder
집은 존재하는 단어 중 가장 아름다운 말이다.

- 벽돌로 집을 세우자. Let's build a house with blocks.
- 더 높이 쌓자. Let's pile the blocks up higher.
- 부서졌어. It's broken.
- 다시 하자 Let's do it again.
- 이제 무너뜨려 봐. Now knock it over.
- 와르르 Clunk, bump, bump
- 네가 뭘 만들었는지 말해 줘. Tell mommy what you made.
- 내가 여기 블록을 놓을 게. I'll put one here.
- 이제 정리하자. Let's put them back in your box.
- 블럭 쌓기 나는 좋아해 I enjoy playing with blocks.
- 나도 그래. Same here.
- 다행이다. Thank goodness.

4. 합체

A good car is one of that stops well.
좋은 차는 잘 멈추는 차다.

- 변신　　　　　　　　　Transform
- 합체　　　　　　　　　Unit
- 쿵 쾅~　　　　　　　　clunk bump clunk bump
- 그의 차가 정면충돌했어요.　He was in a head-on collision.
- 그의 차는 추돌 당했어요.　He got rear-ended.
- 그의 차 측면이 들이 받혔어요. He was hit broadside.
- 그의 차가 박살났어요.　　He got totaled.
- 사이드 브레이크　　　　parking brake
　　　　　　　　　　　　/ emergency brake.
- 핸들　　　　　　　　　steering wheel
- 백미러　　　　　　　　rearview mirror
- 속도 줄여.　　　　　　slow down.
- 너무 빨리 달리고 있어.　It is really going fast.
- 이건 약과야.　　　　　You haven't seen anything yet.
- 교통이 꽉 막혔어.　　　Traffic was at a standstill.

5. 구기지 마

Paper has more patience than people. - Anne Frank
종이는 사람보다 인내심이 많다.

- 색종이 접기 하자.　　　Let's do some origami.
- 뭘 만들고 싶어?　　　　What do you want to make?
- 엄마 배 만들어 주세요.　Mom, make me a boat, please.
- 나도 만들었어요.　　　　I made it, too.
- 엄마가 해주세요.　　　　You do it.
- 네가 해봐. 다시 봐.　　You can do it. Look at it one more time.
- 이렇게 접어.　　　　　　Fold it like this.
- 구기지 마.　　　　　　　Don't crumple it.
- 반으로 접어.　　　　　　Fold it in half.
- 펴 봐.　　　　　　　　　Unfold it.
- 가위 풀 어디 있지?　　Where are the scissors and glue?
- 찾아보자.　　　　　　　　Let's look for them.
- 여기요.　　　　　　　　　Here they are.
- 안전가위로 잘라.　　　　Cut it out with safety scissors.
- 선을 따라가.　　　　　　Fold on the dotted lines.

- 풀로 붙여라.
  Paste it on with glue.
- 테이프로 붙여라.
  Tape it together.
- 긴 방향으로 초록색 색종이를 접어라.
  Fold a piece of green paper the long way.
- 종이 한쪽 면에 악어 모양을 그려라.
  Draw an alligator shape on one side of the paper.
- 긴 주둥이와 두 다리 그리고 긴 꼬리를 그려라.
  Draw a long snout, two legs, and a long tail.
- 접힌 선은 악어의 등이 될 거야.
  The fold line will be the alligator's back.
- 6개의 사선을 그려라.
  Draw 6 diagonal slits.
- 색종이를 펴라.
  Unfold the paper.
- 네가 자른 것의 각각을 뒤집어 접어라.
  Fold over each of the slits you cut.
- 크고 이빨이 있는 입과 눈을 그려라.
  Draw a big toothy mouth and eyes.
- 이빨을 잘라라.
  Cut out the teeth.
- 악어를 장식해라.
  Decorate the alligator.
- 위에서 아래로 반으로 접어.
  Fold it in half, top to bottom.

- 뒤집어
  Turn it over.
- 안쪽을 벌려.
  Open the inside.
- 위쪽을 아래로 가게 해서 양쪽을 잡아당겨.
  Turn it upside down and pull both sides.

* 색종이 놀이 이렇게만 말해도 충분해요.

  - 색종이 접기 하자.   Let's do some origami.
  - 자르세요.   Cut it.
  - 풀로 붙이세요.   Glue it
  - 손으로 찢으세요.   Tear it off.
  - 반으로 접으세요.   Fold in half.
  - 색칠하세요.   Color it.
  - 물감을 칠하세요.   Paint it.
  - 예쁘게 장식하세요.   Decorate it.
  - 그리세요.   Draw it.
  - 펴세요.   Unfold it.
  - 뒤집으세요.   Turn it over.
  - 테이프로 붙이세요.   Tape it.
  - 선을 따라가.   Follow the line.
  - 구기지마.   Don't crumple it.
  - 이렇게 하세요.   Do it like this.

* 놀이 종류

- 총싸움
  Playing cowboys and indians
- 전쟁놀이
  playing war games
- 퍼즐
  putting together a puzzle
- 칼싸움
  playing with swords
- 소꿉놀이
  playing house
- 끝말잇기 놀이
  word game
- 끝말잇기 어때?
  How about a word game?
- 좋아요. 그런데 조금만 할래요.
  OK. But I want to keep it short.
- 등 집고 넘기
  Leapfrog.

6. 물구나무 서

*If you change the way you look at things,
the things you look at change.* - *Wayne Dyer*
사물을 바라보는 방식을 바꾸면, 바라보는 대상이 달라진다.

* 동사

inhale	숨을 들이마시다.
exhale	숨을 내쉬다.
put=place	놓다. 두다.
rest	편안히 놓다.
raise	들어 올리다.
lift	올리다.
straighten	똑바르게 하다.
extend	뻗다.
stretch	팔다리 등을 쭉 뻗다.
sag	처지게 하다.
draw	끌다. 끌어당기다.
point	가리키다.
interlace	깍지 끼다.
clasp	(손 등을) 꼭 쥐다.

E. 놀아요

grasp	움켜잡다.
grab	잡다.
lean	기대다. 기울이다.
touch	~에 닿다.
parallel	평행으로 하다.
limp	절뚝거리다.
cramp	경련을 일으키다.

Fitness exercise

- 눈을 감은 채 심호흡을 하세요.
  Take a deep breath with your eyes closed.
- 차려 자세로 서세요.
  Stand up with your arms at your side.
- 일어서서 다리를 꼬아 보세요.
  Stand up and cross your legs.
- 똑바로 서서 발 사이에 약간의 간격을 두고 양팔을 머리 위로 올리세요.
  Stand straight, feet slightly apart with your arms over your head.
- 물구나무 서라.
  Stand on your hands.
- 몸을 앞쪽으로 굽혀 양 손바닥을 바닥에 대어 보세요.
  Bend forward and touch the ground with both your palms.
- 허리를 굽혀 손가락 끝으로 양발 사이의 바닥을 짚어 보세요.
  Bend forward at the waist and touch the floor with your

finger tips between your fingers.

- 어깨를 약간 앞으로 하고 똑바로 앉으세요.
  Sit up straight with your shoulders slightly forward.

- 등을 똑바로 하고 의자에 앉아 무릎 위에 양손을 놓으세요.
  Sit on the chair with your back straight and put your hands on your lap.

- 등을 대고 누워서 양다리를 똑바로 하고 올리세요. 그리고 나서 엉덩이를 바닥에서 떼세요.
  You should lie on your back, and lift your legs straight above you. Then lift your hips off the floor.

- 등을 대고 누운 후 무릎을 굽히세요.
  Lie on your back with your knees bent.

- 바닥에 배를 대고 엎드리세요.
  Lie on your stomach facing the floor.

- 다리를 모으세요.
  Keep your legs together.

- 엎드려 다리를 바르게 모으고 양손을 머리 뒤에 놓으세요.
  Lie face down with your legs straight and together and your hands behind your head.

E. 놀아요

Body name

leg	다리	Achilles' tendon	아킬레스건
ankle	발목	shank	정강이
knee	무릎		
calf	종아리	thigh	허벅지
whisker	고양이수염	mustache	콧수염
beard	턱수염	goatee	염소수염
color-blindness	색맹	squint	사시
arm	팔	butt	엉덩이
elbow	팔꿈치	thigh	허벅지
forearm	팔뚝	knee	무릎
palm	손바닥	calf	종아리
finger	손가락	ankle	발목
chest	가슴	toe / baby toe	발가락/새끼발가락
stomach	위	sole	발바닥
waist	허리	lap	무릎
spine	척추, 등뼈	weight	몸무게
hip	골반	jaw, chin	턱, 턱 끝
slobber, saliva	(입속) 침	earlobe	귓불
side	옆구리	armpit	겨드랑이
nape	목덜미	tonsils	편도선
anus	항문	booger	코딱지

nostril	콧구멍
the back of the hand	손등
The sole of the foot	발바닥
toe(big toe, second toe, third, fourth, little toe)	발가락
instep	발등

* 난감하지만 많은 어머님들이 궁금해 물어보셔요.

penis	남자의 성기
genitals	합쳐서 생식기
vagina	여자의 부분
sperm	정자
testis, peanut	고환
egg	난자
You cut the cheese.	너 방귀 뀌었구나.

preposition

toward	~쪽으로	Inward	안쪽으로
forward	앞쪽으로	outward	바깥쪽으로
backward	뒤쪽으로	upward	위쪽으로
downward	아래쪽으로		

Dialogue

M : What's wrong?

K : My foot's asleep.

M : You seem to have sat too long with your legs crossed.

K : Yeah! It really hurts.

M : Just give it a good rub. Then, you'll be okay in a minute.

M : 무슨 일이야?

K : 발이 저려요.

M : 다리를 꼬고 너무 오래 앉아 있었구나.

K : 그래요, 정말 아파요.

M : 잘 주물러 봐.

K : 그러면, 몇 분 후에 괜찮아질 거야.

7. 막상막하야

Life is more fun if you play games. - Roald Dahl
인생은 게임을 즐길 때 더 재미있다.

- 우리랑 카드게임 해요.   Let's play cards.
- 카드 두 벌이 필요해.   We need two decks of cards.
- 나도 끼워 줘.   Can I join you? / Count me in.
- 규칙을 설명해 주세요.   Explain the rules.
- 4명이 하기 좋은 게임이야!   A great game for 4 people!
- 내가 카드 나눠 줄게.   I'll deal the cards.
- 모든 사람이 7장을 가져.   Everyone gets seven cards.
- 나머지 카드는 중앙에 둔다.
  I put the rest of cards in the middle.
- 내 차례야.   It's my turn.
- 내 다음이야.   You are next.
- 같은 패에서 이 카드를 맞춰야 하나요?
  Do I have to match this card in the same suit?
- 난 이렇게 짝을 많이 맞췄어.   I got this many matches.
- 내가 이겼어.   I won.

- 이제 카드 섞자. Let's shuffle.
- 누가 선을 할래? Who wants to deal the cards?
- 내가 선이야. I'm first. / I go first.
- 네가 돌릴 차례야. It's your turn to deal.
- 좋은 패인데. This is a good hand.
- 게임에 몇 팀이 필요해요?
  How many teams do you need for a game?
- 적어도 4팀이 필요해요. We need at least 4 teams.
- 내가 너랑 한 팀 할게. I'll join you for a team.
- 주사위 굴려. Roll the dice.
- 누가 먼저 가는지 보자. See who goes first.
- 뭔가 불공평해 보여.
  Something doesn't seem fair. / Something looks unfair.
- 양자택일해 You can't have cake and eat it too.
- 동전 던져 결정하자. Let's toss for it.
- 막상막하야. It's neck and neck.
- 이 자리 앉아도 되니? Is this seat taken?
- 가능성은 반반이야. It's a toss-up.
- 정반대입니다. It's the other way around.
- 예상외의 결과였어. It was an upset.
- 그냥 재수가 좋았어. That was just a fluke/ I just got a lucky.
- 그냥 비긴 걸로 해. Just call it even. / Just call it a tie.

8. 체인이 빠졌어요

Life is like riding a bike.
To keep your balance, you must keep moving.
- Albert Einstein
삶은 자전거를 타는 것과 같다. 균형을 유지하려면 계속 움직여야한다.

- 나가서 자전거 타자.
  Let's go for a bike ride.
- 이야 재미있겠다.
  That sounds great.
- 인도에서는 타면 안 돼.
  You can't ride on the sidewalk.
- 엄마 놀러 나가요.
  Mom, let's go out to play.
- 잠깐만
  Hang on.
- 헬멧 써야겠다.
  I'll get my helmet.
- 안전 규칙은 꼭 지켜야 되요.
  Always keep the safety rules.
- 헬멧은 항상 써야 해.
  Always wear your helmet when you ride your bike.

- 항상 차와 사람 조심해.
  Always watch out for cars and other people.
- 자전거 타고 공원에 가도 되나요?
  Can I ride to the park down the street?
- 롤러스케이트 타자.
  Let's go rollerskating.
- 나한테 맞게 자전거 안장을 조정해야겠어.
  I need to adjust the seat to suit me.
- 자전거 안장, 팔꿈치 및 무릎 보호대, 보조 바퀴
  saddle, elbow and knee pads, training wheels
- 브레이크를 조여 줘야겠는데.
  The brakes need to be tightened.
- 체인이 빠졌어요.
  The chain came off.
- 아빠 체인을 다시 끼울 수 있어요?
  Daddy, can you put the car chains back on?
- 타이어 펌프로 공기를 넣어야 되요.
  I have to pump in some air with the tire pump.
- 나는 균형을 못 잡아서 넘어져요.
  I lose my balance and fall.

9. 꼼짝 마

A guilty conscience needs no accuser.
도둑이 제 발 저리네.

- 꼼짝 마.   Freeze / Don't move.
- 손들어.   Hands up.
- 벽에 서.   Against the wall.
- 다리 벌려.   Spread your legs.
- 총 내려놔.   Put down your gun.
- 넌 이제 체포됐다.   You're under arrest.
- 손들어.   Put your hands up, please.
- 너희는 독안에 든 쥐야.   You're trapped like rats.
- 엎드려.   Deck the cover. Get down.
- 먼지 하나 없이 다 내놔.   Down with dust.
- 숨은 의도가 뭐지? / 무슨 꿍꿍이야?   What's the catch?
- 손 내려.   Put your hands down.
- 저리 비켜.   Get out of my way.
- 명중   Bull's eye

13.
중등부 Class 1

*Behind every young child who believes
in themselves is a parent who believed first.*
자신을 믿는 아이 뒤에는 먼저 그 아이를 믿어 준 부모가 있다.

* 선생님 선택이 까다롭고 얌전한 중1 남학생, 의대 입학

항상 선생님을 선택하는 게 어렵다는 어머님과의 상담 후, 만난 중1 남자아이는 너무 얌전하고 하얀 피부와 말이 없는 아이였다. 방에는 엄청 큰 거북이, 조그만 햄스터 두 마리가 있었다.

거북이를 청계천에서 사왔을 때는 손바닥만 했던 거북이가 지금은 등짝이 솥뚜껑보다 커졌단다.

아빠가 병원장이시라 아들을 의대에 꼭 보내고 싶다는 말씀을 들었고, 전교 1, 2등을 유지하는 데 영어 문법과 독해가 2개 정도 늘 틀린다고 했다.

그리 어려운 건 아니었기에 학생이 틀리는 문제의 이유를 찾으면 될 것 같았다. 하지만 그보다 학생이 선생님과 마음을 여는 게 먼저

었다. 관심사를 보니 내가 오히려 더 궁금해서 이것저것 물어보고 수업 중에 대화를 하다 보니, 부끄럼이 많고 선한 아이라 어렵게 하는 아이는 아니었다. 다만 학생이 선생님을 선택하는 기준이 믿을 만한 성품의 사람인가를 보는 것 같았다.

수업을 하다 보니 생각 외로 바르게 큰 아이들일수록 이런 기준이 높은 것 같다. 선생님 행동이 예의에 어긋나거나 마음에 안 들거나 관심사 등 수업 외의 것을 많이 따진다. 특히 사춘기가 오는 초등에서 중학교 사이의 학생들은, 특히 더 까다로운 것 같다. 아마도 교과서와 현실의 부조리에서 오는 불협화음에 적응이 힘들어서가 아닐까 싶다. 세상이 워낙 험하니 이해된다. 나 또한 세상이 험해서 조심하고 의심하는 그런 부분이 있듯이.

드디어 가볍게 만점을 계속 받게 될 때쯤 그만하려고 어머님께 말씀드렸다. 어머님은 "선생님은 또 다시 만나면 되지 않을까?" 말했는데, 아들이 꼭 나랑 하겠다고 해서 수업을 고3까지 하게 되었다. 선생님을 믿고 좋게 봐줘서 너무 고맙고 선한 학생. 늘 주위 분들이 "KEETS(키츠) 학생들은 왜 다 인상이 좋지?" 하던 말이 생각난다.

나 또한 공부만 생각하는 거친 아이들이 아니라, 성품 교육도 소중하게 생각하는 좋은 어머님들과 좋은 아이들을 만날 수 있어서 무척 기쁘다.

지금은 아마 어디선가 하얀 가운을 입고 진료를 하고 있으리라.
그 선한 성품으로 좋은 일 많이 하는 명의가 되길 바란다.

14.
중등부 Class 2

* 중1에 만나 사춘기를 음악으로 풀며 서울대 음대 입학.

모든 길이 힘들지만 음악 전공으로 대학을 가는 아이들은 어떤지 몰랐었다. 그런데 수업을 해보며 공부만 힘든 줄 알았는데, 그들의 길이 어떤 전공보다도 힘들구나 싶었다.

약간만 잘못해도 다른 소리가 나고, 불규칙적인 레슨 시간과 그날의 감정, 같은 동작으로 연주를 반복함으로써 몸이 힘들기도 하고, 혼자만의 공간에서 자기와의 싸움을 해야 하는 것이 무척 힘들다고 말한다. 밖에서만 볼 때는 몰랐는데, 직접 아이들을 수업을 해보면서 알게 되었다.

어떤 면에서 공부는 같은 과목을 친구들과 어울리며 함께 고생하는 것이라면, 예술은 일찍부터 친구들과 다른 길을 선택해 혼자만의 공간에서 자기와의 싸움을 해야 하는 것이 심리적으로 무척 힘든 것 같았다. 그런 아이들이 모인 예중, 예고는 더 힘들다는 걸 수업 오는 학생과 학부모를 통해 알게 되었다.

입시 경쟁에서 예술은 노력만으로는 안 되는 것이기에, 절대 음감의 능력, 쉼도 음악을 들어야 힐링이 되는 아이가 아니면 너무 고통일 것 같았다. 그러기에 그 길을 선택하고 달려가는 길에 부모와 가족의 많은 배려가 필요할 것 같았다. 그래도 그 과정이 지나고 나면 가장 큰 상으로 보답하니 견뎌내는구나 싶었다.

악기를 하는 친구들은 시간이 부족하지 학습 이해도는 누구보다 뛰어난 것 같았다. 한 번 설명하면 규칙을 찾듯 금방 이해하고, 문제를 푸는 능력이 뛰어난 것 같았다. 다만 학습 시간을 빼기가 쉽지 않은 것 같아 안타까웠다. 갑작스런 교수님들과의 레슨 일정으로 영어 수업 시간이 늘 일정할 수 없었다.

수업에서 만난 음악 하는 아이들은 공부하다가도 너무 힘들면 "선생님, 잠깐 좀 쉬었다 하면 안 되나요?" 하며 자신의 악기와 관련된 음악을 듣는다. 그때 그 아이의 얼굴에서 스트레스가 사라지는 걸 보고, 이런 아이가 음악을 하는구나 싶었다.

무대에 서면 그냥 너무 행복하다는 아이.

음악을 들으면 평화가 밀려온다는 아이.

음악만 하면 좋겠다는 아이.

드디어 그 힘든 시간을 지나 자신이 가장 원하던 최고의 대학교 음대를 찾아갔다.

꿈을 이루기까지 엄마와 아이가 감내해야 했던 인내와 수고, 그들이 흘렸을 눈물을 생각하며 존경의 마음을 전하고 싶다.

이제 어디선가 멋진 공연을 준비하고 있으리라.

15.
고등부 Class

* 과학고 1학년 남학생, 고려대 입학

"KMO 상은 어떻게 하면 받니? 정말 대단하다" 했더니, "그냥 학원에서 선생님이 시키는 대로 하루 8시간 하면 되요."라고 답하며 대단하지 않다고 말하던 학생.

다섯 살 늦둥이를 위해 KEETS 수업에 오셨다가 고1 큰아들을 내게 부탁하셨다.

수학을 하느라 상대적으로 영어에 시간을 투자하기가 쉽지 않았다고 한다. 어머님이 이런 학습 방법의 영어 수업을 알았더라면 어릴 때 시작했을 텐데, 하는 후회가 된다고 하셨다.

그 당시 과학고 영어 수업이 대학교 영문과 수업처럼 영어 원서 소설과 졸업을 위한 토플 점수가 있어야 된다고 해서 두 가지를 같이 병행해 준비해야 했다. 수학, 과학만으로도 힘들 텐데, 영어까지 최고로 요구한다니 정말 힘들겠구나 싶었다.

기숙사 생활이라 시간이 없어 주말 4시간씩 2일을 활용할 수밖에 없었다. 놀고 싶은 마음이 얼마나 많을까 싶은 주말이지만, 그동안 수학으로 다져진 학습 태도라 빠지지 않고 오는 성실하고 얌전한 학생이었다.

부끄럼 많은 남학생이었지만 자기 분야의 두꺼운 과학 책을 얘기할 때면 눈이 반짝이고, 지식 전달을 너무 잘하는 걸 보고 이런 멋진 아들은 보고만 있어도 행복하시겠다 싶었다.

암기해야 할 단어와 독해가 서툴렀지만, 꾸준함이 통했는지 2년반을 치열하게 강행군을 했다. 그동안 다른 아이들이 어릴 적에 하던 영어 시간 투자를 수학에만 투자해서 서툴고 속도는 약했지만, 수학 공부의 집중력처럼 착석 시간이 길고 한결같은 노력이 통했던 걸까. 학생은 자신이 원하던 학교, 원하던 학과에 합격했다.

좋은 결과로 졸업할 수 있어서 정말 기뻤다. 대학 입학하고 물어보니, 영어로 강의가 이뤄져 처음에는 걱정했었는데 지금은 대학교 강의를 큰 어려움 없이 잘 따라가고 있다고 해서 더 기뻤다. 그때는 영어 난이도가 워낙 높아 수업을 엄청 많이 힘겹게 진행해야 했는데, 지나고 보니 추억이 되어 잘했구나 싶다.

F.
내일 학교 갈 준비

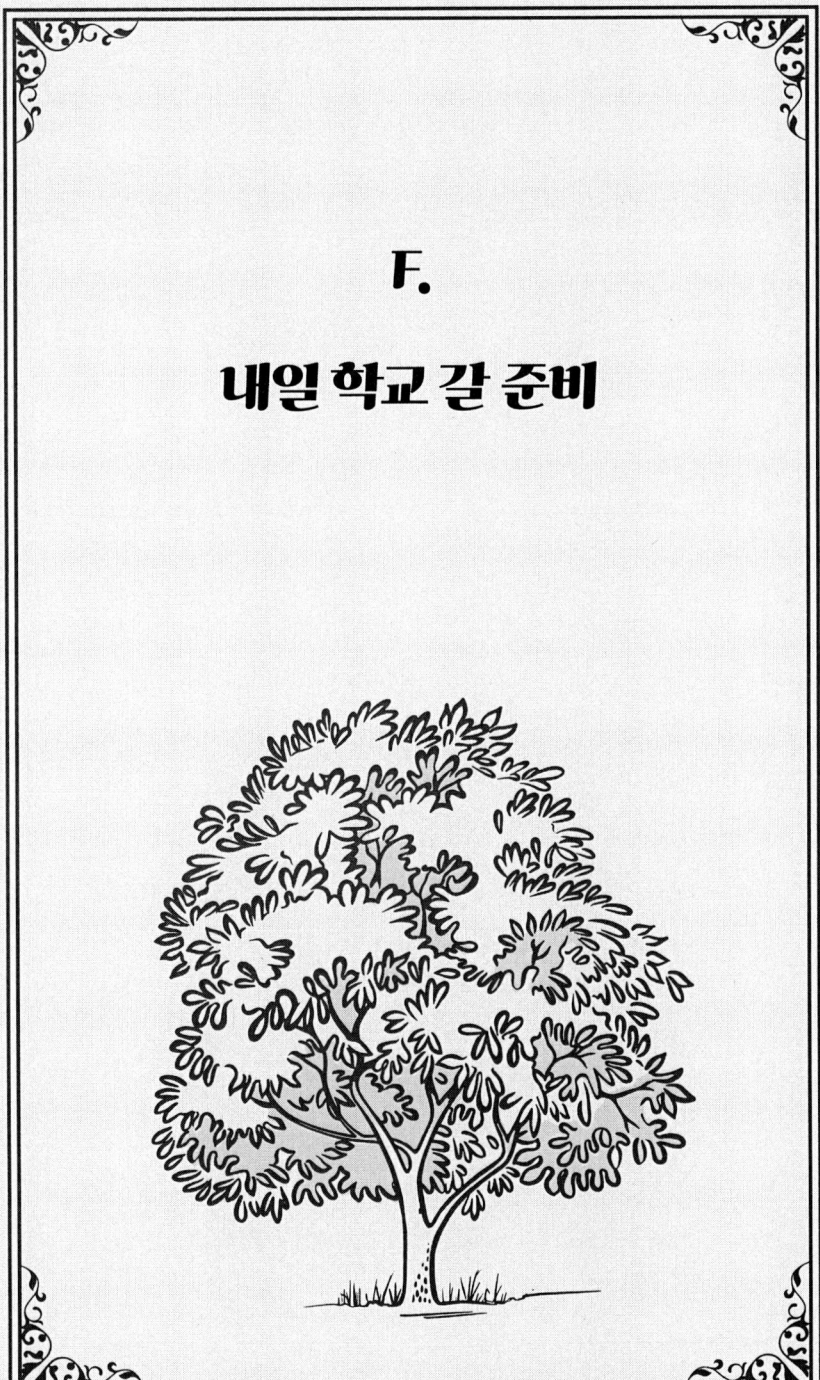

1. 게임 좀 그만해

Lost time is never found again
- Benjamin Franklin
잃어버린 시간은 다시 찾을 수 없다.

- 게임 그만해. Stop playing computer games.
- 이제 쉴 시간이야. Time to take a break!
- 이제 막 이기려고 하는데. I'm about to win.
- 5분만 더해. Five more minutes.
- 소리 좀 줄여줘. Turn down the volume, please.
- 저녁시간이야. 꺼줄래? It's dinner time. Turn it off.
- 숙제 다하면 게임하게 해줄게.
  If you finish your homework, I'll let you play games.
- 오늘은 이만하면 충분해.
  That's enough for today.
- 얼마나 더 할 거야?
  How much longer are you going to play?
- 컴맹 computer illiterate.
- USB에 저장했니?
  Did you save it on your USB memory stick?
- 자료를 모두 날려 버렸어. I lost all my files.

- 처음부터 다시 해야겠어.
  I need to start over.
- 상처 입은 마음을 감싸 줄 수 있어.
  I can fix broken heart.

Dialogue

K : Oh no!

M : What happened?

K : While I was working on my essay, my computer crashed!

M : Did you save your work?

K : No, I lost all my files.

M : That's a real pity.

K : 이런!

M : 무슨 일이야?

K : 숙제를 하고 있었는데, 컴퓨터가 다운되었어.

M : 작업한 것 저장했니?

K : 아니, 자료를 모두 날려 버렸어.

M : 정말 안됐구나.

2. 방이 엉망이네

Outer order contributes to inner calm
- Gretchen Rubin
겉이 정돈되면 마음도 평온해진다.

- 엉망이네!
  What a mess!
- 청소기 돌려라.
  Vacuum the room.
- 방 쓸어라.
  Sweep the room.
- 걸레로 바닥 닦아라.
  Clean the floor with a rag./Mop the floor.
- 가구 먼지 치워라.
  Dust the furniture.
- 방을 정리 정돈해라.
  Set the room in order.
- 쓰레기통 비워.
  Empty the trash can.
- 쓰레기통 내놔라.
  Take out the garbage.
- 옷들을 옷장에 걸어라.

Hang the clothes up in the closet.

- 바닥에 있는것 다 주워.
  Pick up everything off the floor.

- 장난감 치워.
  Put the toys away.

- 네가 어지른 건 네가 치워.
  If you make a mess, you clean it up!

- 원래 자리에 갖다놔.
  Put them back in their place.

- 필요 없는 것 버려.
  Get rid of the unnecessary things.

- 흩어져 있는 장난감들 정리해.
  Arrange the toys which were scattered.

- 방을 말끔하게 정리했어요.
  I tidied up the room.

- 피아노에 있는 먼지 닦아.
  Dust the piano.

- 화분에 물 줘.
  Water the plants.

- 탁탁 털어!
  Shake it off!

3. 식탁에 수저 놓아라

A shared meal is a shared life.
한 끼를 함께 한다는 것은 삶을 함께 한다는 것이다.

- 엄마 부엌일 좀 도와줄래?
  Can you help mom out in the kitchen?
- 식탁 닦아라.
  Wipe the table.
- 식탁에 수저 놓아라.
  Place the spoons and chopsticks on the table.
- 반찬을 놓아라.
  Put the side dishes on the table.
- 밥을 퍼라.
  Put the rice into the rice bowls.
- 국을 퍼라.   Ladle the soup.
- 컵에 물을 따라라.   Pour water into the glasses.
- 식사 후 식탁 위 치워라.   Clear the table after the meal.
- 깨끗이 닦아라.   wipe up the table.
- 국물이나 맑은 국   broth
  국 전체 or 스프   soup
  찌개처럼 진한 것   stew

4. 정전이에요

A blackout reminds us how bright life really is.
정전은 우리 삶이 얼마나 밝았는지를 깨닫게 한다.

- 전등이 깜빡거려요. The light is flickering.
- 전구가 나갔어요. The light bulb has burned out.
- 정전이에요. We had a blackout.
- 전기가 나갔어요. The electricity is out.
- 따뜻한 물이 안 나와요. There is no hot water.
- 문이 꼼짝도 안 해요. The door is stuck.
- 비디오 고장났어요. The VCR is broken.
- TV가 잘 안 나와요. The TV reception is poor.
- 세면대가 막혔어요. The basin is clogged.
- 변기가 막혔어요. The toilet is clogged.
- 자물쇠가 고장났어요. The lock is broken.
- 배터리가 다 되었어요. The Battery is dead.
- 배터리 충전해야 되요. The battery needs charging.
- 움직이지 않아. It isn't working.
- 손전등 flash light
- 소화기 fire extinguisher

5. 엄마는 형아 편만 들어요

Laughing out loud.
크게 웃어 버려.

- 싸우지 말고 사이좋게 놀아라. Be nice to each other.
- 형아가 때려요. The big brother is hitting me.
- 동생이 나를 방해해요.
  The little brother keeps bothering me.
- 못하게 해주세요. Make him stop doing that.
- 앞으로 나와. Come out to the front.
- 형아 방해하지 마. Don't bother your brother.
- 엄마는 형아 편만 들어. You always take his side.
- 착한 아이는 그러는 거 아냐. A good boy does not do that.
- 동생이 꼬집어요. He pinched me.
- 동생이 깨물었어요. He bit me.
- 동생이 책을 찢었어요. He tore my book.
- 엄마가 둘이 싸우면 어떻게 한다고 했지?
  What did I tell you about quarreling with each other?
- 방에서 못 나온다고 했어요.
  You said we would be grounded.

- 명심할게요. I'll keep in mind.
- 한 번만 용서한다. I'll forgive you just one time.
- 이제 안 그럴게요. I won't do it ever again, mom.
- 너희들이 그렇게 행동하면 엄마는 속상해.
  It hurts my feelings when you act like that.
- 참을 수가 없어요. I can't stand it.
- 변명하지 마. Don't make excuses.
- 오해하지 마. Don't get me wrong.
- 더 이상 참을 수 없어. I can't stand him.
- 날 화나게 했어요. He made me angry.
  / He pissed me off.
- 네가 상관할 바 아냐. None of your business.
- 나 오늘 저기압이야. I'm under the weather today.
- 네가 뭘 의미하는지 알겠어. I think I know what you mean.
- 그 말 취소해. Take it back.
- 내버려 둬. Let it lie.
- 너한테 달렸어. It's up to you.
- 고자질하지 마. Don't tattletale.
- 난 너랑 절교야. I'm through with you.
- 가서 싸워. Go fight.
- 너, 나랑 얘기하기 싫다 했잖아.
  You said you won't talk to me.
- 망설이지 말고 사과해.
  Don't hesitate and apologize to him.

F. 내일 학교 갈 준비

- 사과해. Apologize to him.
- 부끄러운 줄 좀 알아라. Shame on you.
- 너답지 않다. That's not like you.
- 그건 좀 너무하다. (선을 넘는 말이나 행동을 할 때)
You are crossing the line./You're crossing a boundary.
- 난 널 탓하지 않아. I don't blame you.
- 벙어리가 됐니? Has the cat got your tongue?
- 치사해.
That's so small-minded.
That's unfair / That's not cool / That's petty
- 너무 했어.(엄하게 혼냈을 때) You went too far.
- 긁어 부스럼 만들지 마. Don't ask for trouble.
- 당했지롱! 딱 걸렸어. (You got) busted!
- 내 장난감 망가뜨렸어. 너 혼 좀 나 봐라.
You broke my toys. You are in big trouble.
- 형아가 나 놀려요. He is teasing me.
- 형아가 찼어요. Brother kicked me.
- 형아가 내 손을 밟았어요. Brother stepped on my hands.
- 형아 왜 그랬어? Why did you do that?
- 동생이 놀렸어요. He teased me.
- 왜 놀렸니?
Why are you teasing your brother?
- 형아가 장난감 같이 안 놀려고 해서요.
He doesn't want to share with me.

- 장난감 이리 내놔.
  Give me the truck.
- 다른 사람을 따돌리는 건 안 좋아.
  It's not good to pick on others.
- 서로 잘 안 놀면 장난감 뺏을 거야.
  If you are not good to each other, I'll take the trucks away from you.
- 사돈 남 말 하고 있네.
  Look who's talking.
- 뻔뻔스럽게도 형아가 날더러 멍청하다고 말했어요.
  He had nerve to tell me that I was stupid.
- 아빠가 많이 화났어. 그러니 내가 잘 말해 줄게.
  Daddy is very upset. So I'll go and talk to him for you.
- 말해 봤자 소용이 없어.
  Don't waste your breath.
- 기가 막혀서.
  I was stunned.
- 당근이지. 당연하지.
  You bet.
- 욕하지 마.
  No cursing. / Don't swear.
- 네가 놀리는데 넌더리가 났어.
  I've got enough of your teasing.
- 제정신이 아니었어요.
  I got carried away.

F. 내일 학교 갈 준비

- 진짜로 혼 좀 나야겠구나.
  You really need to be punished.
- 선착순
  First come, first served

Dialogue

M : Why do you have long face?

K : I had a fight with (형아 이름~).

M : What was it about?

K : He teased me.

B.B : I didn't mean it.

M : So, now do you regret it?

B.B : Yes, I was just upset and I took it out on him.

M : Then, say sorry to your little brother.

M : 왜 그렇게 시무룩하니?

K : 형아랑 싸웠어요.

M : 무엇 때문에 싸웠어요?

K : 날 놀렸어요.

B.B : 진심은 아니었어요.

M : 그럼 이제 그 말을 후회하니?

B.B : 네, 그냥 화가 나서 그에게 화풀이를 했어요.

M : 그럼 미안하다고 해라.

6. 이빨이 흔들려요

Sour grapes.
못 먹는 감 찔러나 본다.

- 이빨이 흔들려요.
  My tooth is getting loose.
- 이빨이 빠졌어요.
  My tooth fell out.
- 네 이빨 이리 줘.
  Hand me your tooth.
- 가서 입 헹궈라.
  Go rinse your mouth (out).
- 오늘 밤에 그것을 베게 밑에 두렴.
  Put it under your pillow tonight.
- 네가 자는 동안 이빨 요정이 방문할 거야.
  Your tooth fairy will visit while you're sleeping.
- 내가 이빨 요정에게서 뭘 받게 되죠?
  What will I get from the tooth fairy?
- 아마 1 달러.
  Probably 1 buck.

- 내일 아침까지 못 기다리겠어요.
  I can't wait until tomorrow morning.

- 우와 돈 벌었어.
  Wow! I got money.

- 덧니   side tooth

  사랑니   wisdom tooth

  틀니   dentures

  영구치   permanent tooth

- 8incisors+8molars+4canines=20 baby teeth

- 앞니   incisors / front teet

  어금니   molar

  송곳니   canine

  앞어금니(송곳니와 어금니 사이) bicuspid/premolar

  젖니   baby tooth

  앞니   front tooth(incisor)

- 잇몸   gum

- 앞니를 교정하고 싶습니다.
  I 'd like to have my front teeth aligned.

- 치열 교정기   braces

7. 속으로 읽어

The more that you read, the more things you will know.
- Dr. Seuss
많이 읽을수록, 더 많은 것을 알게 된다.

- 책 읽어 줄까?
  Do you want me to read you a book?
- 네가 고를래?
  Do you want to pick out the book?
- 장화 신은 고양이 읽어 주세요.
  Read me the 'Puss in Boots.'
- 속으로 읽어.
  Read it to yourself.
- 책 읽을 시간.
  It's story time.
- 잠잘 시간.
  Time for bed.
- 잠이 안 와요.
  I'm not sleepy.
- 나도.
  Me, either.

- 아침에 일찍 일어나야 해.
  You have to get up early.
- 꼭 껴안고 책 읽자.
  Let's cuddle and read.
- 같이 읽을 짧은 책 하나 골라 와.
  Go pick a short storybook we can enjoy together.
- 한 개로 통일해.
  Agree on one book.
- 이불 속에 들어가.
  Go under the covers.
- 어떤 이야기 읽어 줄 거예요?
  What story are you going to read me tonight?
- 밤새고 싶다.
  I want to stay up all night.
- 그 책 다 읽었니?
  All done with the book? / Are you done with the book?
- 소원을 빌어 봐.
  Make a wish.
- 누워서 눈감고.
  Lie down and close your eyes.

8. 이 책에 감동 받았어요

Once you learn to read, you will be forever free.
- Frederick Douglass
한 번 읽는 법을 배우면, 영원히 자유로워진다.

- 책이 지루해요.   The book is boring.
- 책이 우스꽝스러워요.   The book is silly.
- 책이 드라마틱해요.   The book is dramatic.
- 책이 웃겨요.   The book is funny.
- 책이 무서워요.   The book is dreadful.
- 책이 환상적이에요.   The book is fantastic.
- 책이 이해하기가 어려워요.
  The book is difficult to understand.
- 책이 내가 읽기에는 어려워요.
  The book is difficult for me to read.
- 책이 너무 재미있어서 나는 하루 종일 읽었어요.
  The book was so interesting that I read it all day long.
- 그 책은 읽을 만한 가치가 있었어요.
  The book was worth reading.
- 그 책은 나에게 가장 영향력이 있었어요.
  The book had the most influence on me.

- 그 책은 나에게 많은 정보를 가르쳐 주었어요.
  The book taught me a lot of information.
- 나는 그 책에 감명 받았어요.
  I was impressed by this book.
- 나는 내 친구에게 그 책을 읽도록 추천하길 원해요.
  I want to recommend my friends to read the book.
- 나는 그 책을 통해 놀라운 일을 알게 되었어요.
  I learned something amazing through the book.
- 이야기가 싱거워.(이야기가 강렬함이나 흡입력이 없을 때)
  The story is wishy-washy.

Dialogue

M : Where were you after school?

K : I was on the playground riding my bike.

M : I'm not that naive, you know?

K : Oh, mom! Why won't you believe me?

M : Because you told a lie last time.

K : But mom, I've decided to turn over a new leaf.

엄마 : 방과 후에 어디 있었니?

아이 : 자전거 타느라 운동장에 있었어요.

엄마 : 엄마가 바보인줄 아니?

아이 : 엄마! 왜 날 안 믿으세요?

엄마 : 왜냐하면 지난번에 네가 거짓말했잖아.

아이 : 하지만 엄마, 나 새사람이 되기로 결심했어요.

9. 빨래 접자

That's a piece of cake.
식은 죽 먹기.

- 빨래 해보자.
  Let's do the laundry.
- 분류하자.
  Let's separate the light and dark clothes.
- 세탁기에 넣자.
  Let's put it in the washing machine.
- 세제 양을 재어 보자.
  Let's measure the laundry detergent.
- 시작하자.
  Let's start the washing machine.
- 끝날 때까지 기다리자.
  Let's wait until it's done.
- 빨래 널어라.
  Hang the clothes on the clothesline.
- 툭툭 털어 널자.
  Let's shake it out and hang it up.

- 이제 빨래 걷자.
  Let's take it down.
- 빨래를 접자.
  Let's fold the laundry.
- 제자리에 갖다 두자.
  Let's put it all away.
- 서랍장에 양말 넣어 줘.
  Please put your socks in your drawer.
- 엄마 위해 심부름해라.
  Run an errand for mom.
- 아빠 세차하시는 것 도와드려라.
  Help your dad wash the car.
- 빨랫줄   clothes line

  빨래집게   tongs

  옷걸이   hanger

  건조대   clothes rack

  세탁기와 건조기
  Washing machine and dryer(washer dryer)

G.
사시사철 쓸 수 있는 말

1. 안개꽃은 영어로 뭐에요?

It's a pie in the sky.
그림의 떡.

- 봄이 가까이 왔네.
  Spring is around the corner.
- 새순이 파릇파릇 돋아나네.
  Fresh shoots are budding and turning green.
- 나뭇가지에 벚꽃 좀 봐.
  Look at the cherry blossoms on the branches.
- 새들이 노래하네.
  The birds are chirping.
- 뭉게구름 좀 봐.
  Look at the cumulus clouds.
- 나뭇잎이 바람에 살랑살랑 나부끼네.
  The leaves are fluttering in the wind.
- 새싹이 고개를 내미네.
  Little shoots are swaying in the wind.
- 벌에 쏘였어요.
  I was stung by a bee.
- 달콤한   Mellow   풋나기의   callow

버드나무	willow	베개	pillow
개나리	golden bell	담쟁이	ivy
이끼	moss	소나무	pine
무궁화	rose of sharon	나팔꽃	morning glory
수양버들	weeping willow	민들레	dandelion
목련	magnolia	진달래	azalea
달맞이꽃	Moon-light flower	안개꽃	baby's breath
강아지풀	foxtail grass		
아지랑이	heat shimmer/heat haze		
춘곤증	fatigue of springtime		

- 봄을 기다리는 'Groundhog day'에 등장하는 표현.

   "If the groundhog spies his shadow,
   "그의 그림자를 땅에서 본다면,

   six more weeks of snow and ice.
   6주 더 눈과 얼음이 올 거고.

   If no shadow the groundhog sees,
   그림자를 보지 못하면,

   Soon will blow a warm spring breeze."
   따뜻한 봄바람이 불어올 거야."

G. 사시사철 쓸 수 있는 말

2. 푹푹 찌네

Don't count your chickens before they hatch.
김칫국물 마시지 마.

- 날씨가 점점 더워져요.
  It is getting hotter and hotter.
- 후덥지근해요.
  It is humid.
- 끈적거리는 날씨.
  It's sticky.
- 푹푹 찌네요.
  What a sizzler!
- 지독하게 더운 날씨야.
  It's scorching hot.
- 눈이 부셔서 눈을 못 뜨겠어요.
  The sun is shiny so I can't open my eyes.
- 더위를 더 이상 못 견디겠어요.
  I can't stand this heat any longer!
- 난 더위를 잘 타.
  I'm sensitive to the heat.

- 샤워할래요.
I'll take a shower.

- 팥빙수 먹고 싶어요.
I want to have crushed ice with sweet red beans.

- 선풍기 꺼.
Turn off the electric fan.

- 나는 부채질했다.
I fanned myself with a paper fan.

- 더위 빨리 끝났으면 좋겠다.
I hope this hot weather ends soon.

- 비가 빨리 멈췄으면 좋겠다.
I hope the rain lets up soon.

- 쮸쮸바, 아이스바, 아이스크림
freezer pop, popsicle, ice cream cone

- 삼계탕
chicken broth with ginseng, rice and jujube

- 에어컨
air conditioner

- 땀띠
heat rash

- 땀띠약
heat rash powder

- 어떻게 더위를 극복하니?
How do you beat the heat?

- 냉방병
air conditioning sickness

G. 사시사철 쓸 수 있는 말

- 막바지 더위
  late summer heat
  Indian summer(가을이 시작된 뒤 갑자기 더워지는 시기)
- 비가 억수 같이 와요.　　It's raining cats and dogs.
- 눈이 부셔요.　　　　　　It is so bright.
- 수영복　　　　　　　　　swimsuit / bathing suit
- 이열치열　　　　　　　　fight fire with fire

Dialogue

Kid : Mom, I got something on my back. It hurts. Could you look at it?

M : Sure, let me see. Ah, it's a heat rash.

Kid : I've been sweating a lot after school.

M : Yeah, that's why. I'll help you. It's no big deal. First take a shower.

Kid : 엄마, 등 뒤에 뭐가 난 것 같아요. 아파요. 좀 봐줄래요?

M : 그래, 어디 좀 보자. 아~ 땀띠 났네.

Kid : 학교 갔다 오면 땀이 줄줄 흘렀어요.

M : 응 그래서 그랬구나. 내가 도와줄게. 이건 아무것도 아냐. 먼저 샤워해.

3. 천고마비의 계절

Autumn shows us how beautiful it is to let things go.
- Unknown
가을은 내려 놓는 것이 얼마나 아름다운지 보여준다.

- 가을에는 하늘이 높고 푸르네요.
  The sky is extremely clear and blue in fall.
- 온도차가 심하네.　　　The temperature varies a lot.
- 쌀쌀하네.　　　　　　It's chilly.
- 산들바람이 부네.　　　A gentle breeze is blowing.
- 나무들이 단풍 들었네.　The trees turned red and yellow.
- 낙엽 밟자.　　　　　Let's crunch through the fallen leaves.
- 추수의 계절.　　　　Harvest season.
- 낙엽이 흩날리네.　　　The leaves are scattered by the wind.
- 바람 좀 쐬고 올게　　I'm going to go get some fresh air.
- 가을은 천고마비의 계절이라고 해요.
  The fall is called the season of high sky and plump(stout) horses in Korea.
- 만일의 경우를 대비하라.　Keep the powder dry.
- 장미가시　Thorn　　　밤송이가시　bur
  생선가시　bone　　　나무가시　splinter
  선인장가시　prickle

4. 진눈깨비가 내렸어요

Kindness is like snow-it beautifies everything it covers.
- Kahl Gibran
친절은 눈과 같아서 닿는 모든 것을 아름답게 만든다.

- 날씨가 추워졌어요.   It became cold.
- 추워서 덜덜 떨었어요.   I shivered because of the cold.
- 서리가 내렸네.   It was frosty.
- 첫눈이 오네.   The first snowflakes are falling.
- 눈이 펑펑 오네.   It is snowing heavily.
- 진눈깨비가 내렸네.   It sleeted.
- 눈싸움을 했다.   I had a snowball fight.
- 눈이 녹고 있어요.   The snow is melting.
- 휴대용 손난로   portable hand heater
- 귀마개, 고드름   earplug(earmuffs), icicle
- 살갗이 텄어요.   I got chapped skin.

5. 자가용에서

The road to sucess is always under construction.
- Lily Tomlin
성공으로 가는 길은 항상 공사 중이다.

- 차에 타 / 차에서 내려
  Get into the car. / Get out of the car.
- 벨트 매렴.
  Buckle up. / Fasten your seatbelt.
- 좌석벨트가 꽉 조여 있는지 확인해.
  Make sure your seatbelt is fastened.
- 제대로 앉아 있어요.   Sit up a little, please.
- 편안해?   Are you comfortable?
- 문 닫는 거 잊지 마.   Don't forget to close the door.
- 창문에 기대지 마.   Don't lean on the window.
- 출발 준비 되었나요?   Are you ready to go?
- 운전할 때 조용히 해.   Be quiet while I'm driving.

6. 지하철에서

Life is like the subway-you can always change direction.
삶도 지하철처럼, 방향을 바꿀 수 있다.

- 손 꼭 잡아.
  Hold on tight.
- 우리는 지하철을 기다려야 해.
  We need to wait for the train.
- 내 가까이에 있어.
  Stay close to me.
- 자리 찾아보자.
  Let's find a seat.
- 뛰지 말고 조용히 해.
  Don't run and be quiet.
- 다음 역에서 내리자.
  Let's get off at the next station.
- 조심해, 바닥이 미끄러워.
  Be careful, the floor is slippery.

7. 버스에서

Today's ride shapes tomorrow's you.
오늘의 이동이 내일의 너를 만든다.

- 버스 카드 가지고 있니?
  Do you have your bus pass?
- 앞자리에 앉자.
  Let's sit in the front.
- 자리에 앉아 있어.
  Stay seated.
- 벨 눌러 줄래?
  Can you press the button?
- 거의 다 왔어.
  We're almost there.
- 다음 정류장에서 내려야 해.
  We need to get off at the next stop.

8. 기차에서

If life derails, rebuild the tracks.
삶이 탈선하면, 선로를 다시 깔아라.

- 자리를 찾아보자. 　　Let's find our seats.
- 손잡이를 잡아. 　　　Hold the handrail.
- 기차 타자. 　　　　　Get on the train.

　우리 자리 찾아보자. 　Let's find our seats.
　3호차인 것 같은데. 　I think we're in car number 3
　창밖을 봐. 　　　　　Look out the window.
　나무들이 지나가는 거 보여?
　Do you see the trees passing by?

- 풍경이 너무 예뻐. 　　The scenery is beautiful.

　기차에서 내리자. 　　Get off the train.

9. 비행기에서

Flying might not be all plain sailing,but the fun of it is worth the price.
-Amelia Earhart
비행은 항상 순탄하지는 않지만, 그 즐거움은 그만한 가치가 있다.

- 자리를 찾아보자. Let's find our seats.
- 안전벨트를 매. Fasten your seatbelt.
- 이제 비행기가 올라가고 있어. We're going up now.
- 영화 볼래? Do you want to watch a movie?
- 구름 위를 날고 있어. We're flying over the clouds.
- 곧 착륙하니까 준비해 We'll land soon, so get ready.
- 이륙 중에는 자리에 앉아 있어야 해.
  Stay seated during takeoff.
- 이번 여행은 제주도로 갑니다
  This trip, I'm going to Jeju.
- 무박 2일   2day trip without staying overnight

  1박 2일   2days, 1night

  3박 4일   4days, 3nights

  4박 5일   5days, 4nights

10. 애완동물에 대해 이야기할 때

Let sleeping dogs lie.
긁어 부스럼.

- 이름이 뭐에요?
  What's your pet's name?
- 무슨 종류의 애완동물을 갖고 있니?
  What kind of pet do you have?
- 너의 개는 무슨 종이야?
  What breed is your dog?
- 얼마나 오랫동안 애완동물을 키웠니?
  How long have you had your pet?
- 언제 밥 먹여?
  When do you feed your dog?
- 뭐 먹여?
  What do you feed your dog?
- 너의 개는 어떤 재주를 할 수 있니?
  What kind of tricks can your dog do?
- 그는 막 악수하는 법을 배웠어.
  He just learned how to shake hands.

- 너의 개는 운동을 많이 하니?
  Does your dog exercise a lot?
- 우리는 매일 그를 마당 주위를 달리게 해.
  We let him run around the yard everyday.
- 너의 앵무새는 말할 수 있니?
  Can your parrot talk?
- 너는 애완동물을 수의사에게 얼마나 자주 데려가니?
  How often do you take your pet to the vet?
- 너의 애완동물들이 털갈이를 했니?
  Is your pet going through a molt?
- 너의 개가 집안을 어지럽히니?
  Does your dog make a mess of the house?
- 너의 개가 항상 신발을 물어뜯니?
  Does your puppy always chew up your shoes?
- 개는 기분이 좋을 때면 꼬리를 흔든다.
  When a dog is happy, it wags its tail.
- 나의 고양이는 정말 뚱뚱해. 매일 먹고 자기만 해.
  My cat is really fat. It just eats and sleeps all day.

11. 스타벅스에서

Leave a good scent everywhere.
어디서든 좋은 향기를 남겨라.

- 주문 먼저 하나요, 아니면 자리 먼저 잡나요?
  Do I order first or find a seat first?
- 자리 찾자.
  Let's find a seat.
- 이 자리 누가 있나요?
  Is this seat taken?
- 밖에 앉아도 될까요?
  Can I sit outside?
- 창가에 앉아도 되나요?
  Can I sit by the window?
- 냄새 좋다.
  It smells good.
- 뭐 마시고 싶어?
  What do you want to drink?
- 핫초코 주세요.
  Can I have a hot chocolate, please?
- 쿠키 먹고 싶어요.
  I want a cookie.

- 톨 사이즈 아메리카노 하나 주세요.
  Can I get a tall Americano, please?

- 너무 뜨겁지 않게 따뜻하게 주세요.
  Can you make it warm, not too hot?

- 아이스로 주세요.
  Can I get it iced, please?

- 매장에서 드시나요, 가져가시나요?
  For here or to go?

- 매장에서 마실게요.
  For here, please.

- 포장해 주세요.
  To go, please.

- 케이크도 하나 주세요.
  Can I get a cake, too?

- 얼마에요?
  How much is it?

- 8달러 50센트에요.
  That will be $8.50.

- 카드로 계산할 수 있나요?
  Can I pay by card?

- 현금으로 할게요.
  I will pay by cash.

- 이 쿠폰 사용할 수 있나요?
  Can I use this coupon?

- 여기에 카드를 대 주세요.
  Please tap your card here.

- 스타벅스 카드인가요? Do you have a Strabucks card?
- 영수증 여기 있어요. Here's your receit.
- 좀 붐비네. It's quite crowded.
- 음료 기다리자. Let's wait for our drinks.
- 기다리기 잘했어. Good job waiting!
- 쏟지 않게 조심해. Watch out you might spill it.
- 테이블 깨끗이 하자. Let's clean the table.
- 여기 네 음료야. Here's your drink.
- 한 모금 살짝 마셔 봐. Take a small sip.
- 빨대 하나 주세요. Can I have a straw, please?
- 맛있어 보이네. That looks yummy.
- 사진 찍자. Let's take a picture.
- 네 물건 다 챙겼지? Did you get all your stuff?
- 다음에 또 오자. Let's come again next time!

H.
아가에게 영어로 말하고 싶어요

- 젖 먹여요.   I nurse(feed) my baby.
- 분유 먹여요.   I feed my baby formula.
- 트림시켜 줄게.   Let me burp you.
- 배불리 먹으렴.   Eat all you can.
- 똥 쌌구나.   You pooped.
- 오줌 쌌구나.   You peed.
- 가만히 있어 봐.   Hold still.
- 설사했구나.   You had diarrhea.
- 변비 걸렸네.   You are constipated.

- 옹알이하는구나.   You are babbling.
- 안아줄게.   I'll pick you up.
- 잠투정하지 마.   Don't fuss.
- 뒤집고 싶구나.   You want to turn over.
- 배밀이 하는구나.   You're trying to crawl.
- 음식을 흘렸구나.   You dribbled your food.
- 변기에 가고 싶어?   Do you want to go potty?
- 응가 하러 가자.   Let's go potty.
- 참지 마.   Don't hold it.

I.
뱃속 아가랑 말하고 싶어요

- 안녕 아가 엄마야.
  Hi, sweetheart. It's mommy.
- 발로 차네.
  You are kicking.
- 엄마 아빠 빨리 보고 싶니?
  Are you in a hurry to see mommy and daddy?
- 엄마 아빠도 네가 무척 보고 싶단다.
  We also can't wait to see you.
- 엄마는 너를 갖게 되서 많이 기뻐.
  Mommy is so happy to be expecting you.
- 이제 길 수 있구요.
  You can crawl now.
- 이젠 앉아 볼까?
  Try to sit up now.
- 그래 앉았다. 이젠 안 넘어지네.
  All right, You're sitting up. You don't fall over any more.
- 자장가 불러 줄게.
  I'll sing you a lullaby.

- 앞 / 뒤 / 옆으로 가고 싶니?
  Do you want to go forwards / backwards / sideways?
- 조금만 더.
  Try a little harder.
- 바로 그거야.
  That's how you do it!
- 조심해 넘어질라.
  Be careful! You might fall over.

  저런 넘어졌네.
  Oh no, you fell over.

  괜찮아.
  That's okay.

  다시 해봐.
  Try again.
- 너 침 흘리는구나. 엄마가 닦아 줄게.
  You're drooling. I'll wipe your mouth.

16.
Daily Children Song

음악은 어느 곳에서나 힘든 것을 덜어 주는 가장 큰 힘인 것 같아요. 음악을 가까이 하게 하는 것은 아이에게 또 다른 세상을 향한 아름다움에 눈뜨게 하는 것이겠죠?
똑같이 반복되는 일상을 리듬에 담아 말해 보면 어떨까요?
안 외워지던 표현도 쉽게, 발음 연습과 듣기 훈련도 함께!
34곡을 완전히 외워 자연스럽게 불러 주세요.

- 아침에 일어날 때

  Good morning to you

  Good morning to you

  There're always new places with sunshine in faces.

  Is this not the way to start a new day?

- 안 일어날 때

  Lazy mary, will you get up,

  will you get up, will you get up?

  No, no mother, I won't get up, I won't get up.

No, no mother, I won't get up, I won't get up today.

- 아이 목욕탕에서 씻길 때

    Here we go round the mulberry bush

    the mulberry bush, mulberry bush.

    Here we go round the mulberry bush

    so early in the morning.

    This is the way we brush our teeth,

    Brush our teeth, brush our teeth.

    This is the way we brush our teeth,

    so early Monday morning.

    This is the way we wash our face

    wash our face, wash our face.

    This is the way we wash our face

    so early Tuesday morning.

    This is the way we brush our hair.

    brush our hair. brush our hair.

    This is the way we brush our hair.

    so early Wednesday morning.

    This is the way we put on our clothes.

    put on our clothes, put on our clothes.

    This is the way we put on our clothes.

    so early Thursday morning.

    This is the way we eat our food

    Eat our food, eat our food.

    This is the way we eat our food.

    so early Friday morning.

- '옷을 뭘 입힐까?' 아이랑 고민하면서

  Sally is wearing a red dress, red dress, red dress.

  Sally is wearing a red dress, all day long.

  Sally is wearing black shoes ,black shoes, black shoes.

  Sally is wearing black shoes all day long.

  Sally is wearing blue jeans, blue jeans, blue jeans.

  Sally is wearing blue jeans all day long.

  Sally is wearing a green hat, green hat, green hat.

  Sally is wearing a green hat all day long.

- 밥 먹을 때

  Are you hungry?

  Yes, I am.

  Hungry, hungry?

  Yes, I am.

  I'm hungry. Oh, I'm hungry.

  Oh, I'm hungry now.

  Are you thirsty?

  Yes, I am.

  thirsty, thirsty?

  Yes, I am.

  I'm thirsty. Oh, I'm thirsty.

  Oh, I'm thirsty now.

- 신발 신으며

  One two buckle my shoe

  three four open the door

five six pick up sticks.

seven eight lay them straight

nine ten a good fat hen

- 유치원 버스 타러 나가며

    Walking walking walking walking

    hop hop hop hop hop hop

    running running running running running running

    Now, let's stop. Up and down.

- 학교 예의를 당부할 때

    Oh no, don't do that. (*3)

    It's not ok, now don't do that.

    Don't yell (*3) in the classroom

    Don't fight (*3) in the classroom

- 엄마랑 헤어지면서

    See you later see you soon (*3)

    dancing on my darling.

- 아이가 기분이 안 좋아 보일 때

    Sad (*4)

    you look very sad today

    Sad (*4)

    You look so sad

    Why are you sad?

    Sad (*4)

I am very sad today.

Sad (*4)

I am so sad.

I lost my dog.

- 유치원 갔다 와서

    I went to school one morning and

    I walk like this (*3)

    I went to school one morning and

    I walk like this

    all on my way to school.

    I saw a little rabbit and he

    hopped like this (*3)

    I saw a little rabbit and he hopped like this

    all on my way to school.

    I saw a tall police man and he

    stood like this (*3)

    I saw a tall police man and he stood like this

    all on my way to school.

    I heard the school bell ringing and I

    ran like this (*3)

    I heard the school bell ringing and I ran like this

    all on my way to school.

- 놀이터에서 친구 사귈 때

    How are you my friend, how are you today?

    Will you please come in?

Tra la la la la la la

How are you my friend, how are you today?

Will you please sit in?

Tra la la la la la la

- 친구랑 놀 때

    Come and play with me.

    Everybody plays.

    We will play in perfect harmony. (*2)

    Come and play with me.

    Everybody plays.

    play together as we sing along.

    Come and play with me.

    Everybody plays.

    We will always be friends true and blue.

- 시소에서 놀 때

    See-saw, up and down

    Which is the way to London town?

    one foot up, the other foot down,

    That's the way to London town

- 놀이터에서

    see-saw, see-saw,

    who's on the see-saw?

    See-saw see-saw

    who's on the see-saw?

I see Sandy on the see-saw.

I see Sam on the slide.

See-saw see-saw slide

See-saw, see-saw slide

She saw Sandy on the see-saw.

She saw Sam on the slide.

- 친구랑 헤어질 때

Little friend good bye to you

good bye (*3) to you

May our Lord bless you! (*2)

See you (*3) again, see you again.

- 돌아와 목욕시킬 때.

Rub-a dub-dub

three men in a tub,

and who do you think were there?

the butcher, the baker,

the candlestick-maker;

All going to the fair.

- 엄마가 간식 해줄 때

Pat-a-cake, pat-a-cake, baker's man

Bake me a cake as fast as you can.

pat it and prick it and mark it with B

and put in in the oven for Baby and me.

for Baby and me. for Baby and me.

put it in the oven for baby and me.

- 집에서 블록 쌓기 할 때.

  I'm going to build a little house with a chimney tall,

  a slopping roof-and a garden wall,

  and two tiny windows you can peep inside.

  I'm going to build a table big enough for two,

  Two little chairs-one for me-one for you.

  knock at the knocker, and please come in

  My little house is shining like a bright new pin.

- 미술 놀이할 때

  Draw paint cut it out

  Draw paint cut it out.

- 아이가 조용해서 불안하여 문 열어 볼 때

  What are you doing?

  I'm playing a game.

  Watch what I do and then do the same

  What are you doing?

  I'm playing a game.

  Watch what I do and then do the same

- 엄마랑 쇼핑갈 때

  To market (*2)

  to buy a fat pig:

  home again, home again,

jiggety-jig

To market to market

to buy a fat hog:

home again, home again,

jiggety-jig

To market (*2)

to buy a plum bum

home again, home again,

Market is done.

- 도로에서 주의시킬 때

    Honking horns go beep beep

    Bicycles go ding ding

    Look both ways when you cross

    careful careful of the cars.

    red light telll you to stop.

    Yellow light is on wait.

    The light is turning green

    careful careful of the cars.

- 병원 갈 때

    Miss polly had a dolly who was sick sick sick

    So she phoned for the doctor to come quick quick quick

    The doctor came with her bag and her hat,

    And she knocked at the door with a rat-a-tat-tat

    She looked at the dolly and she shook her head,

    And she said,"Miss Polly, put her straight to bed."

She wrote on a paper for a pill, pill, pill,

"I'll be back in the morning with my bill, bill, bill."

- 아이가 뭘 찾고 있을 때.

    What's wrong Andy?

    I can't find my book.

    What's wrong Andy?

    I can't find my book.

    I can't hear the teacher I can't reach the bookshelf.

    I can't find my pencil.

    I can't see the board.

    Oh, Andy!

    He can't hear the teacher.

    He can't reach the bookshelf.

    he can't find his pencil.

    He can't see the board.

- 아이랑 풍선 놀이할 때

    This is my red balloon

    My red balloon

    Up it goes, pull it down!

    Up it goes. Pull it down!

    This is my red balloon

    my red balloon

- 가족이 함께 놀러 갈 준비하면서

    Hop in the car.

16. Daily Children Song

We're going for a ride. (*2)

Where are we going? (*2)

Hop in the car.

We're going for a ride. (*2)

Are we there yet, daddy?

No, not yet.

Are we there yet, daddy?

No, not yet.

How much longer?

Not much longer.

Oh we're almost there.

Hooray!

Are we there yet, daddy?

No, not yet.

Are we there yet, daddy?

No, not yet.

Are we there yet, daddy?

No, not yet.

But we're almost there .

Hooray!

- 아이랑 놀러 갈 때 차에서

    The wheels on the bus go

    round and round (*3)

    The wheels on the bus go round and round

    all day long

The daddies on the bus go
read (*9)
The daddy on the bus go
read (*3)
all day long
The mommies on the bus go
don't do that (*3)
The mommies on the bus go
don't do that (*2)
all day long
The children on the bus go
wriggle (*9)
The children on the bus go
wriggle (*3)
all day long
The babbies on the bus go
wah (*9)
The babbies on the bus go
wah(*3) all day long

- 놀이공원에서

    Merry go round the sun
    Merry go round the moon
    Merry go round the chimney pots
    on a Saturday after noon.
    Bump!

- 흔들 목마 탈 때

Now rocking-horse, rocking-horse, where shall we go?

The world's such a very big place you must know.

To see all its wonders, the wise people say,

would take us together a year and a day.

- 실컷 놀고 돌아올 때.

The more we sing

together (*3)

The more we sing together

the happier we'll be.

for your friends are my friends

and your friends are our friends.

The more we sing together

the happier we'll be.

- 돌아오는 길 해질 때쯤 되어

Sing your way home

At the close of the day

Sing your way home

Drive the shadows away

Smile every mile

For whatever your room

It will brighten your road

It will lighten your load

If you sing your way home.

- 비오는 날

  I hear thunder, I hear thunder

  Oh! don't you? (*2)

  pitter, patter, raindrops.

  pitter, patter, raindrops.

  I'm wet through.

  I'm wet through.

  I see blue skies.

  I see blue skies.

  Way up high. (*2)

  Hurry up the sunshine. (*2)

  I'll soon dry. (*2)

- 침대에서 잠들 때

  Rosy, my posy, you're sleepy and dosy,

  Come sit upon Grandmother's knee.

  Songs I will sing you, sweet sleep to bring you.

  Come cuddle up cozy with me.

17.
Korean Children Song

어느 날 한 꼬마 아이가 "kite는 구멍이 없고 마름모야!"하네요. 우리나라 것보다 외국 것을 먼저 아는 아이들.

'이게 아닌데…' 하는 생각이 들었습니다.

통역 활동을 하며 '내가 우리 것을 이렇게 몰랐나?' 부끄러워 국사책 외우고, 한국 음식 설명 외우던 생각이 떠오르면서 미국 사탕이 아니라 우리나라 유과를, 미국 노래랑 같은 동급으로 우리나라 예쁜 노래를 번안해 불러 주고 싶었습니다.

아이들의 해맑은 눈망울이 반짝일 때, 더 늦기 전에….

- 무엇이 무엇이 똑같을까?

  I wonder I wonder what are the same?

  Two chopsticks look the same.

  They are the same!

- 산토끼

  Jackrabbit, jackrabbit

  where are you going now

hop, hop, hopping as you run

where are you going now.

- 송아지

    Little calf, little calf, little spotted calf

    mama cow is spotted, too!

    You look like your mom!

- 학교 종

    School bell's ringing ding ding dong

    Let's all gather round

    Teacher's waiting in the class

    for us all to come.

- 나비야

    butterfly butterfly

    Come and fly right over here.

    Yellow and white butterflies

    Come and dance right over here.

- 코끼리

    Mr. elephant's trunk is a hand

    When we give him a snack,

    He gets with his trunk.

- 부뚜막

    There's a little calf

Sitting on clay stove

He begins to cry~

Waaa~ waaa~ my bottom is so hot.

- 눈사람

    Little snowman wears a straw hat

    in the winter time

    his eyebrows look so funny,

    nose is crooked, too

    I'll show you what you look like

    little snowman friend

- 시계

    In the morning clock goes off tick-tock, tick-tock

    In the morning clock goes off tick-tock, tick-tock

    always the same sound, tick-tock, tick-tock

    Clock always works non-stop

- 돼지저금통

    One coin ding ding two coins ding ding

    my little piggy bank is wow heavy now

    hahaha, we are good little kids.

    We all love to save our money

    We are the thrifty kids.

- Clock

    In the morning clock goes tick- tock, tick- tock

In the morning clock goes tick- tock, tick- tock

Always the same sound, tick-tock, tick-tock

Clock always works non-stop.

- 누가 먼저 했나?

Who made it like this like this?

Who made it like this like this?

Who did it before me, before me.

Funny, funny, so funny.

- 솜사탕

Hanging on a tree like a yarn, cotton candy in the wind.

Like white snow, it's so clean, sweetest cotton candy.

Holding mommy's hand going on a stroll,

I ate my cotton candy.

Blow, blow, blow on it, my candy's flying away

my sweetest cotton candy.

- Television

Wouldn't it be great

if I were on TV(X3)

Look at me, sing and dance and look at all my fans.

Wouldn't it be great

If I were on TV(X3)

- 그대로 멈춰라

Dance with me gonna have some fun, now it's time to stop. (*2)

Don't even close your eyes, don't even smile a smile.
Don't even shed a tear, stop right there.

- 비행기

Rising rising airplane

fly away, fly away

Higher, higher fly away

our airplane.

- 사과 같은 내 얼굴

Like an apple is my face.

How I look so beautiful

Eyes are shiny, nose is shiny

and my lips are shiny.

- 어린 음악대

Ba-bam-ba, ba-bam-ba, with your fist.

Ba-bam-ba, ba-bam-ba, blowing on your horns.

We are always a little music band.

We're the best in best in the town.

- 짝짜꿍

In front of mommy, clap clap clap

In front of daddy, clap clap clap

Mommy's worries fade away.

Daddy's wrinkles go away.

- 곰 세 마리

    Three bears living in one house

    daddy bear, mommy bear, baby bear

    daddy bear is chubby wubby

    mommy bear is slender

    baby bear is so cute

    tee-tee tee- tee, there you go.

- 그대로 멈춰라

    Dance with me, gonna have some fun.

    Now it's time to stop!(*2)

    Don't even close your eyes.

    Don't even smile a smile.

    Don't even shed a tear.

    Stop right there.

    Dance with me, gonna have some fun.

    Now it's time to stop.

- 우리 모두 다 같이 손뼉을

    All together come on now, clap your hands. (*2)

    All together come on now.

    Clap your hands and sing along.

    All together come on now, clap your hands.

- 동물 흉내

    Ducks go quack, quack, ducks go quack, quack

    Goats go baa, goats go baa.

17. Korean Children Song

pigs go oink, oink, pigs go oink, oink.

Cows say moo, cows say moo.

- 둘이 살짝 손잡고

Hold your hands together,

spin your partner to your right.

Hold your hands together,

spin your partner to your left.

Touch your knees and bump your shoulders,

clap your hands and clap my hands, too.

Hit your knees and bump your shoulders,

clap your hands and clap my hands, too.

- 바둑이 방울

Jingle, jingle, jingle, jingle, jingle, jingle

My puppy's collar-bell's ringing all the way

Wags his tail so happy to see me…

coming out to see me on my way from school

- 강아지

Puppy dog in my house is

such a pretty dog

When I come home from school

ruff ruff ruff

wagging tail, glad to see me

ruff ruff ruff

- 퐁당퐁당

  Splashing, splashing, throw in the pebbles.

  Let's throw pebbles, don't let her see.

  little stream, go far and wide wiggle and giggle and splash all day

  Sitting across the stream

  planting fresh greens

  Tickle the back of her hand

  soft and light you stand.

- 옹달샘

  Deep in the mountain, far away,

  who will come to drink the spring.

  Deep in the mountain, far away,

  who will come to drink the spring.

  At dawn a bunny wakes rubbing his eyes to rise.

  Came to wash his face, but oh no, little bunny drinks the spring.

- 둥글게 둥글게

  Making a circle now

  Making a circle now

  Turning turning in a circle

  as we dance along

  Let's clap our hands

  Let's sing along

  lalalala have fun as we dance along

  linga linga linga linga linga ling (*2)

  Hand in hand together everybody now.

Have fun as we dance along.

- 고향의 봄

Flowers bloomed in my hometown, long long time ago.
peaches, apples and apricots and pink blossoms , too.
red and violet of the rainbow, flowers paint the town.
I still long to go back to my hometown in the sun.

- 숲속 작은 집

In a cottage in the wood,
a little man at the window stood.
He saw a rabbit running by.
knocking at the door.
'help me, help me,' the rabbit said,
'before the hunter shoots me dead!'
'Come little rabbit, come with me.
Happy we shall be.'

- 반달

Milky way in a clear blue sky, sail boat on the sea.
Cinnamon tree all alone, rabbit is crouching near.
sailing without a sail, and without a mast
watch it glide so smoothly into sunset to the west.

- 나리나리 개나리

Lily lily golden bell
Pluck it hold it in your lips.

Bunch of chicks hop hop hop
spring time outing, off they go.

18.
Answer key

1. Nose-picker / pencil-Chewer / Finger-Licker(Thumb-sucker)

2. Sleepyhead / bed wetter(betsy wetsy) / meal-Skipper

3. Look at the sleep in your eyes.

4. Don't flatter yourself.

5. Don't procrastinate.

6. Switch them.

7. Don't be picky.

8. Matches for sale!

9. mackerel, flounder, sea urchin, ear shell, small octopus, tadpole

10. My nose is stuffed.

11. One times two is two.

12. Bundle up.

13. Suspenders, stocking cap

14. babble, drool, doodle

15. Peach, reddish, tan

16. He has snotty nose.

17. lukewarm, freezer pop, popsicle, icicle

18. Mirror, mirror on the wall who is the fairest of this world?

19. Heavenly maiden and woodcutter

20. dimple, freckle, pimple

21. Get on board.

22. Don't tarry and go straight to school.

23. I feel drowsy.

24. Grandma, What big eyes you have?

에필로그

  늘 이렇게 'KEETS(키츠)영어'는 많은 학생 수보다 한 번 와서 오래 달릴 아이들이 옵니다.
  사람을 제대로 알려면 10년은 만나봐야 알게 되는 것 같습니다.
  아이들이 살면서 세 번은 크게 변화하는 것 같고, 그 세 번이 엄청난 위기로 혹은 전환점으로 자리매김하는 것 같습니다.
  아이의 위기에 큰일이 되지 않게 수정하며 사춘기도 곱게 지나가고, 엄마와 자녀의 큰 인생 진로에 공부 그 외의 간과하게 될 부분까지 고민하려면 객관적인 관점에서 부모 이상으로 볼 수 있는 조언자가 필요한 것 같습니다. 저 또한 그 길에 함께해 주신 소중한 선생님들이 계셨듯.
  늘 너무 객관적이고 냉정한 상담이라 어머님들이 속상해 하기도 하지만, '내가 부모라면…'이라 생각하니 솔직한 상담을 하게 될 때가 많습니다.

KEETS(키츠)영어에 오는 부모님들의 특징은 학습의 중요성은 알지만, 자녀의 성향을 많이 살피고 파악 후, 공부에 지치지 않게 하고 싶고, 성품과 정서적인 교육도 놓치고 싶지 않고, 외국에서도 대학 가서도 연계되는 영어를 자녀에게 주고 싶은 분들이 오시는 것 같습니다.

오랜 고민 후 보내시기에 한 아이의 10대를 온전히 함께 다 보내는 것 같습니다.

해외여행, 해외 생활을 많이 하는 가정으로, 국내 대학, 해외 대학 둘 다 고민하는 자녀.

예술 계통(음악, 미술)의 특별한 재능을 가져 그 길로 가려는 자녀.

수학으로 너무 바빠 상대적으로 영어 시간이 부족한 자녀.

해외 경험이 많은 부모님들이 많아서인지, 책의 소중함을 아시는 분들이 오시는 것 같습니다.

책으로 시작했던 아이들은 학습이 늘어날 때쯤이면 학습 후 책을 읽을 시간에는 편안히 쉬는 느낌이 듭니다.

늘 올 때마다 새로운 책을 접하게 되니, 그 시간이 휴식이 되는 것 같아 저 또한 감사합니다.

아무래도 책은 비용이 많이 드는 일이라 영어유치원이나 학원에서는 대부분 챕터북부터 시작하니, 아이들이 책을 통한 행복한 순간은 많이 놓치는 것 같아 아쉬웠습니다.

학습에만 집중해 이런 과정이 무의미하다 생각하시는 부모님들은 3개월이면 답답해하시며 입시 학원으로 떠나십니다. 그러다 사춘기나 위기가 되면 다시 찾아오시는 분들을 자주 만나게 됩니다.

오히려 어학 전공이나 정서적인 부분을 소중하게 생각하는 부모님,

책을 많이 읽어서 서울대나 전문직으로 갈 수 있었다는 어머님들은 수업을 잘 이해하시고 오래 오시는 것 같았습니다.

디즈니 만화 대사가 성인 영화보다 표현과 영어 수준이 높듯이, 그림책도 난이도가 올라갈수록 단어가 너무 예쁩니다. 그 마음을 꼭 전하고 싶어 어릴 때 오는 아이들일수록 더 많이 읽게 하려고 노력합니다. 그런 친구들에게는 그림도 하나의 소중한 언어이기에 정서적으로 큰 도움이 되는 것 같습니다.

많은 부모님들이 자녀 영어 교육의 길을 몰라 헤매다 시간과 돈을 낭비하지 않길 바라는 마음으로 KEETS(키츠)영어 7 Step 중 2nd 책으로 'A Quartet of Threes'를 출간하게 되었습니다. 이 책으로 많은 분들이 영어회화를 즐겁게 시작하길 바라며, 이 즐거움으로 원서 책과 친해져서 책이 입시의 수단을 넘어서, 지식과 삶을 이어주는 소중한 가교 역할을 할 수 있길 바랍니다.